D0680622

To

_____

From

_____

Grace
for the
Day

Grace for the Day

© DaySpring Cards, Inc.
Published by Garborg's™, a brand of DaySpring Cards, Inc.

Scripture quotations are from the following sources: The
HOLY BIBLE, NEW INTERNATIONAL
VERSION® (NIV)® © 1973, 1978, 1984 by
International Bible Society. Used by permission of Zondervan
Publishing House. The Living Bible (TLB) © 1971 by
permission of Tyndale House Publishers, Inc., Wheaton, IL.
The Holy Bible, New Living Translation (NLT) © 1996 by
permission of Tyndale House Publishers, Inc., Wheaton, IL.
THE MESSAGE © Eugene H. Peterson 1993, 1994,
1995. Used by permission of NavPress Publishing Group.
All rights reserved.

ISBN 1-58061-509-0

Printed in China

Grace
for the
Day

Invitation
to Pray

Let prayer nourish your soul as your meals nourish your body. Let your... prayer keep you in God's presence through the day, and His presence frequently remembered.

E. M. BOUNDS

*Prayer is
the breath
of life to
our soul.*

MOTHER TERESA

*Let us come boldly
to the throne of our
gracious God. There we
will receive his mercy,
and we will find grace to
help us when we need it.*

HEBREWS 4:16 NLT

How vital that we pray,
armed with the knowledge
that God is in heaven....
Spend some time walking
in the workshop of the
heavens, seeing what God
has done, and watch how
your prayers are energized.

MAX LUCADO

Get into the habit of dealing with God about everything.... Swing the door wide open and pray to your Father in secret, and every public thing will be stamped with the presence of God.

OSWALD CHAMBERS

We throw open our doors to
God and discover at the same
moment that he has already
thrown open his door to us.
We find ourselves standing
where we always hoped
we might stand—out in the
wide open spaces of God's
grace and glory.

ROMANS 5:2 THE MESSAGE

This is the glory of the
inner chamber, to converse
with God, the Holy One.

ANDREW MURRAY

Adoration

*P*rayer is a response to the outpouring love and concern with which God lays siege to every soul. When that reply to God is most direct of all, it is called adoration. Adoration is loving back.... In adoration we enjoy God. We ask nothing except to be near Him.

Douglas V. Steere

Praise the Lord, I tell
myself; with my whole
heart, I will praise
his holy name.
Praise the Lord,
I tell myself, and never
forget the good things
he does for me.

PSALM 103:1-2 NLT

The love of the Father
is like a sudden rain
shower that will pour
forth when you least
expect it, catching you up
into wonder and praise.

RICHARD J. FOSTER

Loving Creator,
help me reawaken my
childlike sense of wonder
at the delights of
Your world!

MARILYN MORGAN
HELLEBERG

The Spirit of prayer makes
us so intimate with God that
we scarcely pass through an
experience before we speak
to Him about it, either in
supplication, in sighing…
in fervent requests, or in
thanksgiving and adoration.

OLE HALLESBY

What a wildly
wonderful world,
God! You made it
all, with Wisdom at
your side, made
earth overflow with
your wonderful
creations.

PSALM 104:24,27,51 THE MESSAGE

May your life become
one of glad and unending
praise to the Lord as you
journey through this world.

TERESA OF AVILA

Thanksgiving

True prayer is synonymous with
gratitude and contentment....
How marvelous prayer is
for communicating our
delight with God.

GLORIA GAITHER

Let them give thanks to
the Lord for his unfailing
love…for he satisfies the
thirsty and fills the hungry
with good things.

PSALM 107:8-9 NIV

Thank you, Lord,
for the grace of your love,
for the grace of friendship,
and for the grace of beauty.

HENRI J. M. NOWEN

If it is God who gives prayer, then God often gives it in the form of gratitude, and gratitude itself, when it is received attentively in prayer, is healing to the heart.

ROBERTA BONDI

The Lord is my strength
and my shield; my heart
trusts in him, and I am
helped. My heart leaps
for joy and I will give
thanks to him in song.

PSALM 28:7 NIV

We shall come one day
to a heaven where we shall
gratefully know that God's
great refusals were sometimes
the true answers to our
truest prayer.

P. T. FORSYTH

To wait before the Lord.
Wait in the stillness....
You will hear quiet words
spoken to you yourself,
perhaps to your grateful
surprise and refreshment.

AMY CARMICHAEL

Devotion

You have made
us for Yourself,
O Lord, and
our heart is
restless until it
rests in You.

AUGUSTINE

Love the Lord your
God with all your heart
and with all your soul and
with all your strength.

DEUTERONOMY 6:5 NIV

When you pray,
remember it is the
Lord's face you seek.

CHARLES SWINDOLL

Lord, grant this prayer, that my soul may dwell intent and in awed rapture of Your beauty.

*B*ecause you are my
help, I sing in the shadow
of your wings. *M*y soul
clings to you; your right
hand upholds me.

PSALM 63:7-8 NIV

Cling to the Lord in
prayer! He always hears,
and He will answer.

TERESA OF AVILA

Prayer...is that loftiest experience within the reach of any soul, communion with God.

HARRY EMERSON FOSDICK

Ask Anything in His Name

Prayer enlarges the heart
until it is capable of containing
God's gift of Himself. Ask
and seek, and your heart will
grow big enough to receive
Him and keep Him as
your own.

MOTHER TERESA

You may ask me for
anything in my name,
and I will do it.

JOHN 14:14 NIV

Come and sit and ask Him
whatever is on your heart.
No question is too small, no
riddle too simple. He has all
the time in the world.

MAX LUCADO

The best reason to pray
is that God is really there.
In praying our unbelief starts
to melt. God moves smack
into the middle of even an
ordinary day.

EMILY GRIFFIN

Our prayers are answered
not when we are given
what we ask, but when
we are challenged to be
what we can be.

MORRIS ADLER

God can do anything,
you know—far more than you
could ever imagine or guess
or request in your wildest
dreams! He does it not by
pushing us around but by
working within us, his Spirit
deeply and gently within us.

EPHESIANS 3:20 THE MESSAGE

*P*rayer is not asking.
It is a longing of the soul.

He Hears Every Word

God hears and answers....
His ear is ever open
to the cry of His children.

E. M. BOUNDS

I love the Lord because
he hears my prayers and
answers them. Because he
bends down and listens,
I will pray as long as
I breathe!

PSALM 116:1-2 TLB

Somehow, somewhere, I know that God loves me, even though I do not feel that love as I can feel a human embrace, even though I do not hear a voice as I hear human words....

God is greater than my senses, greater than my thoughts, greater than my heart. I do believe that He touches me in places that are unknown even to myself.

HENRI J. M. NOUWEN

You can talk to God because God listens. No need to fear that you will be ignored. Even if you stammer or stumble, even if what you have to say impresses no one, it impresses God—and He listens.

MAX LUCADO

"You will call upon me
and come and pray to me,
and I will listen to you.
You will seek me and find
me when you seek me with
all your heart. I will be
found by you," declares
the Lord.

JEREMIAH 29:12-14 NIV

Lord, my hands
and my heart are open to
You. I know that You are
utterly trustworthy.

GLORIA GAITHER

In
Solitude

Today, Lord, bless this
place and time that I've set
aside to be with You. And
bless all those I pray for.

PATRICIA LORENZ

When you pray,
go into your room, close
the door and pray to your
Father, who is unseen.
Then your Father, who
sees what is done in secret,
will reward you.

MATTHEW 6:6 NIV

I don't say anything to God. I just sit and look at Him and let Him look at me.

OLD PEASANT OF ARS

There are times when
to speak is to violate the
moment...when silence
represents the highest respect.
The word for such times is
reverence. The prayer for
such times is "Hallowed
be thy name."

MAX LUCADO

$\mathcal{M}$y soul finds rest in God alone; my salvation comes from him. He alone is my rock and my salvation; he is my fortress, I will never be shaken.

PSALM 62:1-2 NIV

*C*ontemplation is nothing
else but a secret, peaceful,
and loving infusion of **God**,
which, if admitted, will
set the soul on fire with
the spirit of love.

JOHN OF THE CROSS

Lord, grant me a quiet mind,
And trusting you, for you are kind,
May I go on without fear,
For you, My Lord, are always near.

Grace for Today and Always

Give me, O God
of my prayer, the grace
to continue waiting for
You in my prayer.

KARL RAHNER

Prayer is the deliberate
and persevering action of the
soul. It is true and enduring,
and full of grace. Prayer
fastens the soul to God.

JULIAN OF NORWICH

God is all mercy and grace—not quick to anger, is rich in love. God is good to one and all; everything he does is suffused with grace.

PSALM 145:8-9 THE MESSAGE

Have you ever thought
that in every action of grace
in your heart you have the
whole omnipotence of God
engaged to bless you?

ANDREW MURRAY

The "air" which our souls
need also envelops all of us
at all times and on all sides.
God is round about us...
with many-sided and all-
sufficient grace. All we need
to do is to open our hearts.

OLE HALLESBY

What God gives in
answer to our prayers will
always be the thing we most
urgently need, and it will
always be sufficient.

ELISABETH ELLIOT

For I will give you
abundant water for your
thirst.... And I will
pour out my Spirit and
my blessings.

ISAIAH 44:3 TLB

Prayer
of
Blessing

To believe that God can reach us and bless us in the ordinary junctures of daily life is the stuff of prayer. You see, the only place God can bless us is right where we are, because that is the only place we are!

RICHARD J. FOSTER

O, God, in
mercy bless us;
let your face
beam with joy
as you look
down at us.

Prayer is...a mine which is never exhausted.... It is the root, the fountain, the mother of a thousand blessings.

JOHN CHRYSOSTOM

The possibilities of prayer
run parallel with the promises
of God. Prayer opens an
outlet for the promises...and
secures their precious ends.

E. M. BOUNDS

I said a prayer for you today
And I know God must have heard,
I felt the answer in my heart
Although He spoke no word.
I asked that He'd be near you
At the start of each new day,

To grant you health and blessings
And friends to share the way.
I asked for happiness for you
In all things great and small,
But it was His loving care
I prayed for most of all.

MONTANA
BRIDES

Welcome to Montana—a place of passion and adventure, where there is a charming little town with some big secrets…

Daisy Harding: A liaison with the best man led to the pregnancy this bridesmaid had always secretly desired. But when the irresistible dad discovered her condition, Daisy felt compelled to name another 'donor', believing that the true father, Ryder Redstone, would only marry her out of duty, not love.

Ryder Redstone: His run-around reputation was fiction, not fact, and he sought something meaningful to do for the rest of his days. Daisy and her baby seemed destiny's answer, though the demure mum-to-be was keeping her child's paternity a secret.

Jordan Baxter: His idle threats lead to action when he holds up the sale of the Kincaid home.

Emma Stover: A visit to mummy dearest, Lexine Baxter, ends with Emma in tears…and Lexine plotting once again.

One
Wedding
Night

KAREN HUGHES

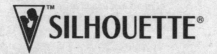

*Silhouette and Colophon are registered trademarks of
Harlequin Books S.A., used under licence.*

*First published in Great Britain 2001.
Silhouette Books, Eton House, 18-24 Paradise Road,
Richmond, Surrey TW9 1SR*

© Harlequin Books S.A. 2000
(original title *It Happened One Wedding Night*)

*Special thanks and acknowledgement are given to Karen Rose Smith
for her contribution to the Montana Brides series.*

ISBN 0 373 04723 1

19-1201

*Printed and bound in Spain
by Litografia Rosés S.A., Barcelona*

KAREN HUGHES

enjoys writing about men and women who want to commit their lives to each other, share dreams and grow old together. She believes romance exists in everyday life and thinks there is a hero inside every man—he just needs the right woman to bring out his best qualities. Wide-open spaces call to her, yet she also likes the bustle and convenience of city life. Experience has taught her that true love can be found anywhere.

To Edie Hanes. For your constant support,
encouragement and friendship. Thank you.

MONTANA BRIDES

Twelve rich tales of passion and adventure,
of secrets about to be told...

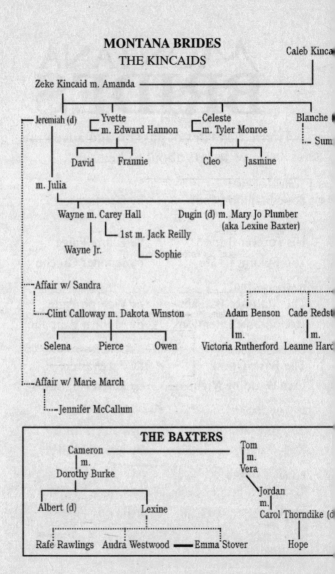

MONTANA BRIDES
THE KINCAIDS

Caleb Kinca—

Zeke Kincaid m. Amanda

Jeremiah (d)

Yvette
m. Edward Hannon

Celeste
m. Tyler Monroe

Blanche

⋯ Sum

David　Frannie

Cleo　Jasmine

m. Julia

Wayne m. Carey Hall

Dugin (d) m. Mary Jo Plumber
(aka Lexine Baxter)

1st m. Jack Reilly

Wayne Jr.

Sophie

⋯Affair w/ Sandra

⋯Clint Calloway m. Dakota Winston

Adam Benson　Cade Redst—

m.

m.

Selena　Pierce　Owen

Victoria Rutherford　Leanne Hard—

⋯Affair w/ Marie March

⋯Jennifer McCallum

THE BAXTERS

Cameron

m.
Dorothy Burke

Tom
m.
Vera

Jordan
m.

Carol Thorndike (d—

Albert (d)　Lexine

Rafe Rawlings　Audra Westwood ━ Emma Stover

Hope

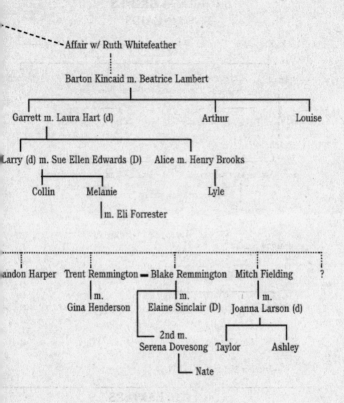

Affair w/ Ruth Whitefeather

Barton Kincaid m. Beatrice Lambert

Garrett m. Laura Hart (d)   Arthur   Louise

Larry (d) m. Sue Ellen Edwards (D)   Alice m. Henry Brooks

Collin   Melanie   Lyle

m. Eli Forrester

Brandon Harper   Trent Remmington — Blake Remmington   Mitch Fielding   ?

m.   m.   m.
Gina Henderson   Elaine Sinclair (D)   Joanna Larson (d)

2nd m.   Taylor   Ashley
Serena Dovesong

Nate

Symbols
..... Child of an Affair
— Twins
d   Deceased
D   Divorced

Prologue

The country music blaring from the jukebox inside the Hitching Post, a popular watering hole on the outskirts of San Antonio, didn't make conversation easy. But Ryder Redstone wasn't interested in conversation. He hadn't been interested in much of anything since the night of his half brother's wedding reception in September. Usually calf roping and the rodeo circuit kept him keyed up, ready to tackle the next competition.

Tomorrow morning he was leaving for California to compete for a substantial purse and a brand-new truck. But even that thought didn't get his adrenaline flowing. It seemed only thoughts of Daisy Harding did. That one night they'd spent together…

Since that night he'd had to frequently shrug off the vision of her face as he'd discovered she was a virgin, as well as the memories of the pleasure that had overtaken them both. A thirty-year-old virgin! At first he'd been astonished, then particularly pleased until he'd awakened to find her gone. Since then, he'd kicked himself up and down. After all, Daisy was his new sister-in-law's sister.

You're spending entirely too much time thinking about a woman you might never see again, he silently admonished himself.

Looking for a distraction, he caught sight of a

blonde standing at the end of the bar. He'd spotted her here a couple of times before. She was a looker, with her curly hair, blue eyes and tight jeans.

Suddenly the bartender yelled for Ryder and pointed to the phone.

Immediately worried that something was amiss with his parents at Rimrock Ranch—he'd told them he was stopping here—he scraped back his chair and strode quickly to the phone.

"How much are you going to win in San Diego this time?" It was his half brother Cade.

He and Cade had their mother's Cheyenne blood in common. Ryder's birth father, who'd been a good father to Cade, too, was also Cheyenne. The bonds of heritage united the family in a way nothing else could. "I'm going to win a shiny crew cab along with enough money to see me through the year."

"Whew! High stakes. How about doing me a favor afterward?"

Cade was the responsible older brother, steady, now married and settled down. The illegitimate son of a deceased Montana landowner, Cade had been called to Whitehorn, Montana, by his newfound grandfather last spring to receive his legacy. He'd decided to stay a month or so to get to know Garrett Kincaid and other members of his family, as well as to forget about a fiancée who'd left him at the altar. Instead he'd met Leanne Harding, married her, and was now building a life there. He wouldn't be asking for a favor if he didn't need one.

"Trouble?" Ryder asked. The Kincaid ranch where Cade was living had seen its share.

"Everything's fine, but I'd like you to come up and start some green colts that I bought. Within the next week or so we're going to have our hands full with calving. You could help out with that in your spare time.''

Ryder laughed. There was no spare time on a ranch, especially not on one the size of the Kincaid spread.

February and March were slow months for rodeoing. He could give Cade some of his time if that's what he needed. ''Sure I can get them started. But don't you have someone to help out?'' Ryder remembered a tall, brooding, blond wrangler who'd kept his distance from Ryder whenever he'd visited Cade.

''I don't like the way he handles the horses. He could learn a lot from you.''

''I'm no teacher,'' Ryder said. ''You know that.''

''Yeah, I know. Everything you do, you do by instinct. But just watching you around the horses might help Watts get the hang of how I intend to handle training around here.''

Ryder planned to leave tomorrow morning to drive to San Diego. Add on five days for the rodeo, another four or five to get back up to Montana. ''I'll be there in about two weeks. Is that okay?''

''That's great. And good luck in California. I'll be watching for that new truck.''

Ryder grinned as he said goodbye, and his gaze rested again on the woman still standing by the bar. Her blue eyes looked into his brown ones as friendly as all get-out. Why sit alone when he could have the company of a pretty woman? And maybe more.

But as he ambled toward her, he saw Daisy Harding's face once more. If his visit to Cade lasted long enough, he might run into her again.

Or he might not.

He told himself it didn't matter.

One

Daisy was still in shock as she parked in front of one of the detached garages on the Kincaid ranch. She'd quit her job and still couldn't quite believe she'd done it!

She laid her hand protectively over her stomach. She'd only started wearing maternity clothes the past few weeks when none of her old clothes would fit. That's when the rumors around the school and among parents had apparently started.

Yesterday, to her dismay and astonishment, Mr. Gladden, the principal of the private school in Sedgemore who had hired her for her specialized skills in teaching reading, had called her up in front of the board of directors. They'd had questions for her. Personal questions. Too personal for her liking and none of their business. The members had asked if she was engaged, if she planned to marry. It was obvious where the inquiries were headed—to dismissal. Her contract contained an ambiguous morals clause the board could interpret however it wanted. So before they could fire her, she'd quit. Upset when she'd gotten back to her apartment, she'd called her sister, Leanne, to finally confide in her that she was pregnant.

Daisy climbed out of her well-worn but reliable SUV, opened the back door and removed her suitcase.

Her recital to Leanne had been met with stunned silence until her sister's usual buoyancy had taken over. Concerned about Daisy and up in arms at a school that would do such a thing, Leanne had invited her to come and stay at the Kincaid ranch for as long as she needed to.

But every time Daisy visited here, she remembered what had happened in a bedroom on the first floor the night an irresistibly sexy cowboy named Ryder Redstone had woven a spell around her.

An icy blast of early February wind tossed Daisy's thick, long brown braid over her shoulder as she walked to the door of "The Mansion," as both her brother Rand, who was foreman on the ranch, and her sister called it. Daisy had no sooner set down the suitcase and pushed the doorbell when Leanne opened the door and enveloped her in a huge hug. After an "I'm glad you're here," she scolded, "You shouldn't have carried that suitcase. I could have brought it in for you."

Leaning back in Leanne's embrace, Daisy studied her younger sister. Leanne's long, wavy chestnut hair fell just below her shoulders. Her green eyes, which looked so much more spectacular than Daisy's brown ones, sparkled. There was an energy about her that always filled a room. Daisy loved her sister dearly despite the fact that she'd felt eclipsed by her ever since Leanne was born. "The suitcase isn't heavy. I didn't bring much."

Leanne studied her, looking worried. "Why didn't you tell me about the baby sooner?"

"Because I didn't want to answer all the questions you'd have."

Leanne shook her head, grabbed the suitcase and

hustled Daisy inside. "Cade's checking the heifers down at the calving barn, but Garrett and Collin are here. There's some trouble about the sale of the property, and they're staying until it's straightened out."

The history of the Kincaid ranch was long and complicated, but when Wayne Kincaid put it up for sale, Garrett, patriarch of the estranged side of the family from western Montana, decided to buy it for seven very good reasons. He'd discovered his deceased son, Larry, had fathered seven illegitimate children. Garrett was still searching for the youngest. As a legacy for the grandchildren he'd never known, he intended to buy the ranch in Whitehorn and give it to them in reparation for things they'd missed all their lives. Cade was one of those grandsons.

"Why is there a problem with the sale?" Daisy asked. "I thought it was a done deal." Last spring Garrett had called a reunion at the ranch, bringing relatives in from far and wide.

"We thought so, too. But some man named Jordan Baxter supposedly found a document that said he had the right of first refusal to buy the place, and he's contesting the sale. Garrett and Collin are fit to be tied."

"But we'll get the whole thing settled." Garrett's strong voice boomed throughout the living room. At seventy-two, he was tall and strong. His Native American heritage was evident in the contours of his tanned face; his blue eyes were welcoming as he strode toward Daisy.

"Leanne said you were coming. You make yourself at home and stay as long as you like." He looked as if he debated with himself about something, but then continued. "Leanne told us you're with child, and I just want you to know there'll be no judgments here.''

Garrett's firm, gentle words brought tears to Daisy's eyes. She'd liked the older man ever since she'd met him at Leanne's wedding. His paternal attitude toward her had made her feel like one of the family. "Thank you."

Garrett cleared his throat. "So you quit your job?"

Apparently Leanne had told him everything. Suddenly she was worried just who knew about her pregnancy. Trying to put that aside for the moment, she answered, "If they don't want me there, I don't want to be there."

"Good for you." Turning, Garrett went to the foyer closet and pulled out a down parka. "I'm going out and give Cade a hand. Do you want me to deliver any messages?"

Leanne grinned at him. "You could tell him I miss him."

Garrett chuckled and shook his head, muttering, "Newlyweds," then headed for the door.

As soon as the heavy wooden portal had closed behind him, Daisy asked, "Just who did you tell about my pregnancy?"

"Cade, Collin and Garrett. Why? Anyone who sees you will know. It looks as if you're five months along." She paused for a moment. "Due in June?"

"Mmm-hmm," Daisy answered vaguely. She certainly didn't want to get into a specific due date with her sister. "You haven't told Rand yet?"

"I tried to call him, but he went into town. Besides, I thought you'd want to tell him yourself."

Rand was the perfect older brother, the perfect first-born. He was strong, athletic, and intelligent, and always did everything right. He'd been foreman on the Kincaid ranch for years. After he'd married, he'd moved into a house on the spread with his new bride and her younger brother. Rand was as proud as he could be of Suzanne and their son, Joe. But Daisy knew he wouldn't be proud of her in her condition. Ever since their parents had died, Rand felt he had to act as a father figure.

"He's going to want to know who the father is." Leanne hooked her arm in her sister's and led her into the living room that was decorated in a Western motif. "I'm curious myself."

Daisy thought about Ryder, about that wonderful night… He might have woven a sensual spell around her, but she wasn't blameless. She'd let herself be seduced because her biological clock was ticking and she'd wanted a child. Before the wedding, she'd seriously thought about finding a sperm donor. But then she'd met Ryder. A few glasses of champagne after Cade and Leanne's wedding reception had loosened her inhibitions. Ryder's kisses, the thought of a baby, and a yearning she'd never experienced before had convinced her that her virginity was outdated and at age thirty she'd better reach for what she wanted or she'd never have it. But when she'd awakened in the middle of the night, naked, lying beside Ryder Redstone, she'd been horrified at what she'd done, slipped out of his room, packed her bag and gone back to Sedgemore.

After she'd discovered she was pregnant, she'd told no one.

Now anyone could see the result of her decision that night, but she wasn't saying who the father was. No one had to know that her new brother-in-law's half brother was the father of this child. Not Leanne, not Cade, and certainly not Ryder. She'd heard about his reputation with women when he'd arrived at the ranch for the wedding. He was a rodeo cowboy who didn't know the first thing about commitment, fidelity or roots. There was another reason, too.

"So are you going to tell me who the father is?" Leanne pressed.

"Lee, I don't want to discuss it, okay?"

After a very long, probing look, her sister nodded. "All right. I won't push for now, but you know Rand will. I invited him and Suzanne for supper. You might as well get it over with."

Daisy realized that if she'd wanted to hole away in seclusion, she should have gone somewhere else. But she knew her family loved her and, after tonight, hopefully they'd just let her figure everything out on her own.

Leanne made Daisy a cup of tea and insisted she eat a biscuit left over from breakfast. The ranch's housekeeper had quit to find work closer to her family in northern Montana, so for the time being, Leanne was taking over the chores.

She showed Daisy to a guest room upstairs. It was the same one Daisy had used when she'd arrived for Leanne and Cade's wedding celebration. The walls were covered with pink rosebud wallpaper. The bed, dresser, washstand and chest were polished dark pine. It was a pleasant room, warmed by the afternoon sun.

"Take a nap while I make supper," Leanne suggested.

"I thought I'd help—"

Leanne waved her offer away. "There'll be time

for that. First and foremost you have to take care of yourself and your baby.''

Daisy's hands went to her belly. ''I intend to take very good care of this child. I love him or her so much already I just can't believe it. I've started reading everything I can find, crocheting booties, buying little toys—'' She stopped.

''I don't think I've ever seen you quite so excited about anything, except maybe teaching. You really want this baby, don't you?''

''I really want this baby.''

Leanne gave Daisy another hug, then left her alone.

Giving in to fatigue that wasn't as bad as earlier in the pregnancy, Daisy fell asleep. When she awoke, she took a shower, then dressed. Never fashion-conscious, knowing she couldn't compete with Leanne, or any of the other pretty girls at school, Daisy had always dressed comfortably, in jeans and large sweaters, skirts and tailored blouses. She'd bought herself new clothes for her pregnancy, but they were comfortable, too. Tonight she wore a long-sleeved, gray sweater with her maternity jeans.

Fortunately, Rand and his family didn't arrive until everyone was ready to sit and eat. When he saw Daisy, a look of astonishment crossed his face. He hadn't seen her since Christmas when loose clothing had hidden any weight she'd gained. But she just hugged his wife Suzanne, kissed her nephew Joe, then took the place Leanne had assigned her at the immense dining-room table. At least five conversations went on around the table at any one time during the meal and Daisy sat back and listened, avoiding her older brother's gaze.

From Collin Kincaid, Garrett's legitimate grandson,

she received a gentle smile that said his attitude toward her was the same as his grandfather's. But after dessert Rand came around the table, took her arm, and said, "Let's go to Cade's office to talk."

"There's nothing to talk about, Rand."

"Who's the father?"

"I'm not discussing the father."

"Does he know?"

"This is *my* baby, Rand."

Her brother drove a hand through his hair. "What's gotten into you, Daisy? Usually Leanne is the wild one, the stubborn one. And how come you're here when school's in session? Are you feeling okay?"

The concern in Rand's voice touched her, and she knew she had to tell him about her job. "I'm fine, but I quit my teaching position before they could dismiss me because of the pregnancy."

After a pause to absorb that, he asked, "How are you set for money?"

Rand was practical to a fault. "I still have my inheritance. And I've been saving a good part of my salary ever since I started teaching. I knew someday I'd want to have a baby. So you don't have to worry about me. Really. Okay?"

Draping his arm around her shoulders, he gave her a brotherly squeeze. "No, it's not okay." After studying her intently, obviously seeing her determination to keep her own counsel, he said, "I'll let you go for now. But I want to know who the father is, and I'll be bringing it up again."

"Leanne's not the only stubborn one," Daisy murmured.

As Cade watched Rand corner Daisy after supper, he followed Leanne into the kitchen. "Did you tell her Ryder's due in soon?''

"No, not yet. I haven't had a chance. Why?''

"Don't.''

Leanne looked at her husband in surprise. "Why not?''

"Because I heard some things after our wedding.''

"Like?'' Leanne prompted, sometimes wishing her husband wasn't the strong, silent type, yet loving him because he was.

Leaning against the counter, he shrugged. "I heard talk that Ryder and Daisy spent some time together. Someone saw them getting pretty chummy after the wedding reception.''

"'Someone'?''

Cade slashed his hand through the air. "It doesn't matter who. You said Daisy's due in June. That would make it about right.''

"Why didn't you tell me this before?'' Leanne asked.

"There was no reason to. Ryder didn't say anything about it.''

"I don't imagine he would,'' Leanne said indignantly.

"Now, wait a minute. Ryder's not the type to hit and run. If he's responsible, if he's the father, he'll do something about it.''

"And you think Daisy will leave if she knows he's coming?''

"It's possible. If he *is* the father, it's better they work things out now.''

Leanne bit her lip. "I don't like keeping it from her.''

Cade shrugged. "She might even leave before he

arrives. You know Ryder. He could get waylaid after the rodeo.''

''You mean, distracted by some woman he meets.''

''I mean, he could look for a new horse or two while he's there, or take his time enjoying the scenery along the way. He said he'll be here, so he'll be here. I'm just not exactly sure when.''

Leanne sighed. No matter what Cade said, she knew Ryder was a ladies' man. Yet she also knew he was as loyal as the night was long and his allegiance to Cade could never be questioned.

Crossing to her husband, she wrapped her arms around his neck. ''I won't say anything to Daisy. We'll let this play out on its own.''

Bending his head, Cade showed his approval by kissing her.

The first week in February passed, and Daisy didn't let her brother corral her again. It really wasn't that difficult. Since ranch work required long hours, everyone was busy most of the time. In the middle of winter, with snow on the ground and calves soon to be born, there was even more to do. She kept to herself mostly and had a few long conversations with Collin, usually about the ranch. He was a lot like Garrett and even resembled him in manner and handsome features. Just like Garrett, he was determined to right his father's wrongs, find his half brothers and treat them fairly. Collin didn't ply her with questions or demand explanations she couldn't give him.

The house was empty Wednesday morning when Daisy heard a truck and horse trailer rolling up the road. She peeked out the window at the shiny blue truck that looked new. It was pulling a battered horse trailer. Not giving it much thought, she went back to her place on the sofa where she held a portable tape player near her tummy playing classical music for her baby. Hearing the front door open, she put the tape player aside. If it was Leanne, she could help her start supper. Cooking for a few hungry males took time.

But when Daisy went into the foyer, she stopped and stared, then almost ran in the other direction.

The oath that came out of Ryder Redstone's mouth scalded her ears. He looked every bit as tall and muscular and devilishly sexy as he had five months ago, but his brown eyes weren't twinkling as he swore again and boomed, "Why didn't you contact me?"

His conclusion didn't have to be the obvious one, she told herself. How she handled this could lead to heartache or it could lead to independence and a life with her child. She chose the independence, wishing she'd worn something other than the nondescript gray top.

"And why would I contact you?" she asked coolly.

He'd been moving toward her, but now he stopped in his tracks. "Why? Look at you! I can't believe Cade or Leanne didn't call me, even if you didn't."

"There was nothing to call about." Reminding herself she had to do what was best for the baby, she said firmly, "This isn't your child."

If he'd looked stunned before, he looked even more shocked now. Then wary. Removing his tan Stetson, he tossed it onto a mission-style table. Without the brim of his hat shading his face, Daisy took a good look at him again. He was at least six-two. His thick, dark brown hair trailed along the collar of his sheepskin coat. His Cheyenne blood gave his face well-chiseled lines, high cheekbones, a determined jaw. But it was his eyes, so dark brown they were almost black, that made something in her soul stir.

"How pregnant are you?"

She told herself she had to be careful, to protect both herself and her baby. Ryder was a rootless rodeo cowboy who used women for pleasure, then moved on. And if that wasn't enough, she could still remember and feel her mother's heartache as she'd told Daisy a secret that Daisy had never shared or forgotten.

"You're not the father, Ryder, let's leave it at that. Rand and Leanne have already put me through the Inquisition." Turning, she started for the living room.

He caught her arm and clasped it firmly but gently. "As well they should. They care about you. A pregnant woman without a husband—"

"What? Can't take care of herself? That thinking belongs in the Dark Ages, Ryder."

She caught his scent as they stood there close together. Man. Winter. Leather. She began to tremble from the scent and sight of him, and she knew she had to get away and get away fast. When she pulled from his grasp, he let her go. She tried to steady her heartbeat as she walked over to the sofa.

He stood, studying her. "Are you staying for the rest of your pregnancy?"

She tried to laugh, but only managed a weak smile. "Goodness, no. I just came for a visit. Why are you here? I thought you'd be…calf roping somewhere." She'd learned he was an expert calf roper when he'd been introduced to her before the wedding.

Rubbing his hand along the back of his neck, he paused for a moment. "I just came from a rodeo.

Cade asked for my help with the horses and calves. He didn't tell you?''

Daisy shook her head. ''Neither did Leanne, but I guess they didn't think it was important. And it's not. I mean…there wasn't a reason for them to tell me. They probably thought I'd be gone before you arrived. Uh, I'm going upstairs and rest for a bit.''

''Are you feeling okay?'' His gaze passed from her bangs and thick braid down her breasts and her overly big top with the noticeable bulge underneath.

''I'm fine.''

His eyebrows arched and he cocked his head. Lifting his duffel bag from the floor, he said, ''I'll come with you.''

''Come with me?'' Her voice went high.

''I saw Garrett outside and he explained Collin is staying in the downstairs bedroom I used the last time I was here and which one upstairs was readied for me.''

The downstairs bedroom. Ryder leading her to it. Kissing her. Drawing her onto the bed. Heat flashed through her that had nothing to do with her pregnancy. In his eyes she saw that he remembered that night, too. Then his gaze dropped to her belly and she backed up a few steps, saying, ''So you're sleeping…''

''Upstairs. Second door on the right.''

She didn't let out her groan of dismay. He was in the room next to hers. No way was she going up those steps with him. No way was she having a cozy conversation with him. No way did she want to be anywhere near him.

''Uh, I think I'll just get a snack in the kitchen. You go on up.''

He frowned. "What about resting?"

Taking a deep breath, she met his gaze. "I'll…rest later. Believe me, Ryder, I can take care of myself." That said, she turned and hurried to the kitchen, praying he wouldn't follow her.

When he didn't, she breathed a sigh of relief.

Maneuvering his saddle to his left arm, Ryder slammed the door of the truck he'd won at the rodeo in San Diego. In turmoil about Daisy, her pregnancy, and her answers to his questions, he strode toward the barn. He'd seen fear then determination flash in Daisy's eyes when she'd spotted him. Why the fear? Why the determination? How likely was it that she'd slept with another man so soon after she'd been with him?

She'd been a virgin, for God's sake. Had she wanted to try out a new sport?

He opened a barn door and headed toward the tack room, trying to sort it out. When he'd first arrived at the Kincaid ranch before the wedding, Daisy had seemed plain, very average, not at all like her enthusiastic and bubbly sister. But as best man, his job had been to entertain the maid-of-honor. He'd found there was a peaceful quality about Daisy, a talent for listening well, and an intelligence that went much deeper than book learning. Then when he'd seen her in her bridesmaid's dress rather than the loose clothing she'd worn the days before, his desire had stirred. He'd flirted with her as he would with any other woman.

Was he the father or wasn't he? She'd said no, but something in his gut told him differently.

Cade was coming out of the tack room as Ryder

made his way toward it. The smells of hay and wood and earth were slightly different up here because of the dampness and the cold. Montana was a different world than Texas, but he felt at home in barns. "I want to talk to you," he barked at Cade, not even bothering with a hello or a handshake upon seeing his half brother. He went into the small room and hung his hand-tooled saddle on one of the pegs.

Cade came to stand in the doorway. "Something wrong?" he asked a little too innocently.

"Hell, yes, something's wrong. Daisy Harding's pregnant."

"Does that have something to do with you?" Cade returned, still in that casually easy voice.

Ryder didn't talk to Cade about women. Private was private. But this situation was different. "Yes, it has something to do with me. She and I—" He cleared his throat, embarrassed for the first time in his life when it came to talking to his brother. "After your wedding reception, we…uh, celebrated together."

"You bedded her?"

Ryder felt a flush creep into his cheeks. "Yeah, but she was plenty willing, believe me. You know I won't touch a woman who isn't."

"Daisy's different," Cade said in a slightly scolding voice.

"Don't I know it. She was a virgin."

Surprise played over Cade's features for a moment. "I shouldn't be surprised. Leanne told me she's always been quiet, keeping to herself and her studies. What are you going to do about it?"

Ryder knew his brother's stake in this: he didn't want to see his wife upset.

"Daisy insists I'm not the father. What has she said to you and Leanne?"

Cade shook his head. "She hasn't said anything. She won't discuss the father. I suspected it might be you. Gil Watts told me you two were pretty chummy after the wedding. I thought maybe he was just trying to make trouble. He has a prejudice against Indians that's hard for him to hide. I've tried to ignore it because he's a hard worker and he stays out of my way. But with you here now—"

Ryder had felt hostile looks from Watts at the wedding, but he and Cade had experienced that kind of thing before. He always tried to let it roll off his back. Besides, Watts was inconsequential right now. "If Daisy won't admit I'm the father, I'm not sure how to handle this. Somehow I have to get at the truth."

"Didn't you use protection?"

"I don't know what happened that night. It's the first time—" He stopped. "That's never happened before."

Cade's gaze disconcerted Ryder, as did the implied question because he couldn't answer it.

"There are lots of reasons why she might not want to admit it," Cade stated factually. "She heard about your reputation before you arrived. I think Leanne warned her you were 'good with the ladies.'"

Ryder frowned. "No wonder she wouldn't talk to me the first day I was here."

"Yeah, well, apparently you won her over."

"Is that criticism?"

"Maybe. What you do has never affected me before, at least not where women are concerned. But now…"

"I'll do the right thing, Cade. I'll take responsibility for this if it's my responsibility. But I can't do that if Daisy isn't honest with me.''

"With both of you under one roof, honesty might come a little easier.''

Ryder hoped his brother was right, but he wasn't so sure. That look of determination in Daisy's eyes had been unyielding. Yet he didn't know a woman he couldn't thaw. Daisy Harding was no exception. He'd get to the truth—one way or the other.

Supper was good, but Ryder had to push the food down with an effort. The table was noisy with talk about calving and horses. Leanne sent him scolding, pointed looks every now and then, so he knew Cade had discussed the situation with her. Daisy avoided him altogether, which annoyed him and made him angry. Not to mention the fact that she was sitting next to Collin Kincaid and accepting conversation from him as if they'd been talking all their lives. Just how long had *that* been going on? Then there were Garrett's appraising glances...

All of it made Ryder damn uncomfortable.

Over coffee, the sale of the ranch came up again and the table went quiet. Collin said, "When I went into town this afternoon, I stopped in at the Hip Hop.''

Ryder knew the Hip Hop Café was the pulse of Whitehorn, Montana. If you wanted to know what was happening to anybody in the town, that's where you went to find out.

Collin went on, "Jordan Baxter happened to be there. He was talking like he was running for an election or something. He was bragging about how he's contesting the sale. The town gossip told me his hate for the Kincaids goes all the way back to when Jeremiah Kincaid had an affair with his mother." Collin shook his head. "If revenge is his motive, he's not going to give up easily."

"Neither are we," Garrett said in a deep voice that brooked no refusal. "I'm not going to let a man filled with hate cheat my grandsons out of their inheritance."

After spending time around Garrett last fall, Ryder had gained great respect for the man. He was determined to do what was right, as any true man would.

What was right.

Finally, after coffee was finished and members of the family dispersed, Ryder cornered Daisy by the buffet. "You and I need to have a talk."

Her eyes grew wide and he almost reached out to tuck in a few hairs that had escaped from her braid. He never imagined he'd be attracted to a pregnant woman, but he'd never imagined being a father, either.

"I told you before, there's nothing to talk about," she said softly.

She was going to be stubborn about this and as contrary as a yearling. So maybe he had to go at this from a side angle. "Cade and Leanne are concerned about you."

Her gaze locked on to his. "I see. Well, they needn't be."

"*I'm* concerned about you."

He saw her swallow and take a small breath. "You needn't be."

There was a scent that always seemed to surround Daisy. At first he'd thought it was his imagination that he'd smelled strawberries. But when they'd made love, he'd realized it was her skin. Must be the kind of lotion she used. They were standing very close. Basically he had her trapped between a high-back wooden chair and the buffet. If she was really involved with another man, she wouldn't abide his touch.

Reaching out, he stroked his thumb over her cheekbone and felt her tremble. Deep satisfaction, along with desire, rushed through him. "Be honest with me, Daisy. You've never slept with anyone but me, have you?"

For a moment he thought she'd tell him. But then her shoulders squared, her chin lifted, and she pushed the heavy wooden chair at her back out of her way. "You know, Ryder, you'd better accept the fact that you're not the only man in any woman's life. According to my sources, you don't know what it's like to date only one woman.

"I had a great time that night, but it didn't mean any more to me than it meant to you. The next day I moved on, just as I imagine you did. So I appreciate your concern, but I have a life and you're not part of it." With that, she turned and practically ran from the dining room.

Just as with the horses Ryder trained when he read body language and signals too subtle for some other folks, he knew Daisy's running meant something. But before he could go after her, Leanne stepped into his path.

"Maybe you'd better let her alone."

"I can't. I think she's carrying my child," he admitted.

"I can't believe you took advantage of her. I can't believe—"

He put a hand up to stop her. "Hold on a minute. She's old enough to know what she wants. She's old enough to know what she was doing."

Some of Leanne's anger ebbed. "I'm worried about her, Ryder. She quit her job over this."

"She what? Never mind. I'll get it out of her somehow. Look, I'm sorry about all this. If you want to give me a good kick where it hurts most, feel free."

At that, a small smile slipped onto Leanne's lips. "It's hard to be mad at you when you're standing in front of me and being so reasonable. Still, I'd better warn you, when Rand finds out you're the one who deflowered his sister, you'd better run for the Crazy Mountains."

"I don't run, Leanne. Problems don't go away because you ignore them. So if you'll excuse me, I think it's best if I go see Rand now and get everything out in the open. But nothing's going to get settled until Daisy tells me the truth."

There was admiration in Leanne's eyes. He didn't want her admiration. He wanted Daisy to let him in. "I'll see you later," he said to Leanne and headed for the closet, his jacket and his hat.

Two

Pacing her bedroom, still trembling from her encounter with Ryder, Daisy glanced at the books and reading materials on the corner of her dresser. She'd stuffed them into her suitcase reflexively. Usually she spent spare moments jotting down new ideas, planning upcoming lessons, thinking of new ways to engage students. Now she didn't know when she'd be teaching again, let alone what was going to happen tomorrow. One thing was painfully clear—she'd have to leave in the morning. She couldn't stay under the same roof with Ryder.

A soft rap on her door startled her. "Who is it?" she called, aware that a six-foot-two rodeo cowboy could be lurking anywhere.

"It's Leanne."

Daisy opened the door. "I was just going to come find you."

"For a sisterly chat or a specific reason?"

"It's kind of you to invite me to stay here, but I'm going to go back to my apartment tomorrow."

Leanne came into the room and sat on the bed. "I had a talk with Ryder. He thinks he's the father of your baby."

"I can't believe he told you—"

"So he *might* be the father?"

Daisy was silent a few moments as she thought

about her answer. Leanne was a mover and a shaker. If Daisy confirmed Ryder's paternity, Leanne would do everything in her power to get them together. That wouldn't be good for her, her baby or Ryder.

"I already told him he's not the father."

Obviously trying to take a gentle approach, Leanne responded, "I'm surprised anything happened between the two of you. You're so different. I know Ryder's one of the sexiest cowboys around, but you usually run from his kind. What made you succumb?"

Daisy felt as if she were caught in a web that was getting stickier by the minute. "Leanne, it happened. That's it."

"Then you slept with someone else soon after?" Her sister looked incredulous at the thought.

"I appreciate your concern, but I really don't want to talk about this."

Her sister studied her intently. "It might be embarrassing for you to stay under the same roof as Ryder after a one-night stand, but if you leave, it's going to look suspicious, and he'll believe even more surely that he's the father."

There was a sparkle in Leanne's eyes that made Daisy wary, but her sister did have a point. If she left, Ryder might think she was afraid to be around him. He might think she certainly did have something to hide. On the other hand, if she stayed, at least for a little while, and stood her ground, she might be able to convince him otherwise. The best thing for her to do was to find another job and find one quickly. Then she would have a good reason to leave.

"Maybe you're right. I wouldn't want him to think I was running from him."

"No man should have the power to chase you from where you want to be," Leanne agreed.

"Do you think Cade would mind if I worked on the computer in his office?"

"I'm sure he wouldn't mind. Do you need it for something in particular?"

"My résumé."

"Are you sure you want to look for work before the baby's born? If you need money—"

"Money's not the problem. But I love my work, Leanne, and there's no reason I can't do it while I'm pregnant."

Standing, Leanne crossed to the door. "I understand. I think Cade's in his office now. I'll tell him you want to use the computer later or tomorrow. And, Daisy?"

"What?"

"Ryder is trouble for most women, so be careful, okay?"

Shrugging as if she could care less about Ryder Redstone, Daisy said, "He's just another cowboy. That night was a mistake. I won't compound it with another."

But after Leanne closed the door behind her, Daisy sank down onto the bed, remembering everything she'd felt that night, remembering the way Ryder had made her feel.

He's just another cowboy, she told herself again.

But she was having trouble believing it.

Insomnia was one aspect of pregnancy that Daisy wasn't used to yet. She was learning that instead of tossing and turning, it was better to get up and do something. Sleep sometimes came faster that way.

She'd stayed in her room for the evening, not wanting to run into Ryder. Everyone on the ranch usually turned in early. She'd heard Garrett come up and settle in his room around nine. Collin, she'd quickly learned, usually turned in around the same time. Leanne and Cade had taken a bedroom suite on the first floor for privacy's sake. That left Ryder. She'd hoped she'd simply missed the sound of his boots coming up the stairs while she was taking a bath.

Reaching for a maroon long-sleeved caftan that would see her through her pregnancy, she slipped it over her nightgown. It was soft and comfortable and zippered down the front. With it, she pulled on a pair of fuzzy black socks and went downstairs. Stopping in the kitchen for a glass of milk and a cookie, she had her snack, then went down the short hall off the living room to where Cade's office was located. If she used the computer now, she wouldn't be in anybody's way. When she flipped on the hall light, she saw that the door was closed. She crossed to it and opened it, thinking she'd find the room vacant.

To her surprise and dismay, Ryder sat at the L-shaped oak desk in front of the computer. When he saw her, his gaze passed over her slowly and she felt naked in the soft flannel, though she didn't know why.

"You're up late," he remarked.

"So are you."

He shrugged. "I don't need a lot of sleep."

She turned to leave. "I won't bother you."

But before she took a step he was on his feet and around the desk. "I'm just checking rodeo schedules online. Nothing important. What do you need?"

Looking up at him with his brown hair falling rakishly across his brow, his shoulders so broad, the snaps of his shirt open at the neck, she was all too aware of needs she had denied for a lifetime until she'd met Ryder.

"I was going to use the computer, but it can wait until tomorrow."

His brows arched as if he was waiting for an explanation. But she wasn't giving one.

His dark eyes continued to probe hers. "What for?"

She gave a resigned sigh. "My résumé. The board at the school where I was teaching disapproved of my pregnancy, and I didn't want a firing on my record, so I quit."

"What are you going to do?"

"I can tutor children until the baby's born if I can't find anything else."

As she talked, Ryder's gaze had drifted to her lips and she now felt as if the two of them were standing entirely too close. When he reached out, she knew she should step away, but something in his eyes kept her feet pinned to the floor.

His thumb gently caressed a spot above her lip. "Crumbs," he said, his voice coarse.

The feel of his callused thumb on her skin sent shivers down her back.

The silence between them stretched until Ryder asked, "Do you know how to use Cade's computer?"

"He showed it to me over the holidays. He has a word processing program I'm familiar with. That's what I'm going to use."

Ryder walked over to the monitor and keyboard. "I'll shut down the browser, then it's all yours."

Cade's office was a nice size, but with Ryder in it,

Daisy thought it seemed much smaller than the last time she'd been here. "You said you were looking at rodeo schedules. When's your next one?"

He pressed a key and gazed up at her. "I'm not exactly sure. It depends how long Cade needs my help. I'm registered for one in Denver in April."

She was hoping he'd be leaving sooner. She'd never expected him to stay around that long. "Surely Cade won't need your help till then."

"That depends. The heifers will start calving any day now. The older cows in about two weeks. Then there are the colts Cade bought."

Ryder faced her and she could almost feel his body heat, could smell the male scent of him. "Trying to get rid of me?"

Her mouth went dry and she remembered being held in his arms. She remembered too much. "No, of course not."

He took a step closer until her socks touched the tips of his boots. "So you don't care how long I stay?"

"Why should I? It's none of my concern."

Reaching out, he took her braid in his hand and ran his thumb over the ends of her hair. She swore she could feel it all the way to her soul.

"What did you say his name was?" Ryder asked.

"Who?" Her voice didn't even sound like hers, and she realized her heart was racing and her hands were trembling.

"The baby's father."

His words were like a splash of cold water. He wasn't just sinfully sexy, he was dangerous, too. Stepping back, she said, "It won't work this time, Ryder."

"What?" He looked genuinely puzzled.

"That look of yours, the low voice, the attention that makes a woman think she's special. I might have fallen for it once, but I won't fall for it again." Then she crossed to the door, saying, "I'll work on the computer tomorrow. Good night."

When the door closed behind Daisy, Ryder felt as if he'd had the wind knocked out of him. She made him sound like an uncaring S.O.B. who consciously charmed women to get what he wanted. He wasn't like that.

Was he?

Granted, he usually got what he wanted without much trying. It had always been that way. He'd learned early on that a compliment here and a smile there got him a lot further than anything else. But he'd never thought of it as anything more than flirting, a prelude to a dance men and women shared before they coupled. The trouble was, that coupling had taken a different turn with Daisy. Ever since that night, he'd felt…changed in some way.

He still didn't know what about her got to him, why he enjoyed talking to her, why his blood rushed hotter the more they were together, even in her present condition.

And that condition concerned him.

When Rand Harding had learned Ryder had bedded his sister, Ryder could tell Daisy's brother had wanted to tear him limb from limb. Ryder couldn't blame him. If he had a sister, he'd be just as protective. But he'd also told Rand if Daisy wouldn't admit he was the father, he couldn't force her to accept his support.

Somehow he had to get closer to her.

Somehow he had to make her admit the truth.

* * *

Ryder was used to Texas and heat and winters that were more wet than frigid. But Montana was another story. As he checked the heifers in the pasture beyond the calving barn, he glanced up at the gray sky, wondering when the next snowfall would come. He knew up here they prayed for dry weather above zero, but they didn't always get what they prayed for.

Jimmy Mason joined him in the pasture. They'd worked together earlier this morning from the back of a pickup, feeding cattle. Jimmy walked with Ryder toward a group of cows gathered around the stand of cottonwoods. If any of them were far along in labor or having trouble, they'd have to move them to the calving barn.

Jimmy's coppery hair was almost covered by his black Stetson. His nose and cheeks were red from being out in the cold and wind. Ryder had met Jimmy last fall. At twenty-one, the young man still had a lot to learn about ranching, but he was willing to learn.

"Cade told me the colts he bought are coming in this afternoon," Jimmy said.

Jimmy didn't usually initiate conversations. The youngest of the hands, he was shy and kept to himself. So Ryder knew he must have mentioned the colts for a reason. "Around two, I was told," Ryder answered.

"Can I help?"

"You mean, unload them?"

"No. Work with them. I heard Cade talking to Gil. He said you don't use ropes or nasty ways to break them."

Ryder gave one of the heifers a pat on the rump. "I don't break horses, Jimmy. I start them."

Jimmy thought about that. "Can I learn?"

Ryder had seen Jimmy around the animals; he gave them the respect they deserved. "I don't see why not. If Rand can spare you." Rand set up the assignments for his men.

"I'll ask him at lunch," Jimmy said with a smile.

Everyone who worked on the Kincaid ranch ate lunch at the bunkhouse. Ryder thought about Daisy back at the house. He'd prefer having lunch with her, but it was important he spend time with the men if he was going to get along with them. He didn't think there would be any problems except for Gil Watts, but maybe he was borrowing trouble when there wasn't any. Maybe they'd just stay out of each other's way.

The remainder of the morning sped by, and Jimmy and Ryder joined the rest of the men for sandwiches and plenty of hot coffee in the bunkhouse. Afterward they went their separate ways, attending to the various aspects of running a ranch. Ryder was walking toward the calving barn to check on a calf that had been born that morning, when he caught sight of Daisy and Leanne coming toward him.

"A little cold for a walk, isn't it?" he asked them.

"I needed some fresh air, and Leanne insisted on coming along," Daisy explained, her dark green jacket zipped tightly over her belly. She was wearing earmuffs and a scarf around her neck and looked as cute as could be.

Leanne motioned to the path in the snow. "I was afraid she'd fall."

"If you have things to do, I can show her what's happening," he offered.

Daisy protested, "I don't need a tour guide" at the

same time as Leanne said, "Sounds like a good idea to me."

Before either of them could blink, Leanne had started off back toward the house. Ryder suspected she was aiding and abetting him so he could get at the truth. He was thankful for that. Offering his arm to Daisy, he said, "C'mon, I'll show you around. The action's just starting."

She hesitated a moment but then took his arm.

He motioned to the corral south of the calving barn. "There are about five hundred bred heifers there. One or two of the hands check them every half hour to see if they're ready to calf or already have. If we catch them in time, we take them into the barn and watch them, and if they're having trouble, then we help."

Just then, Jimmy came out of the smaller barn and saw Daisy. He blushed and mumbled, "Afternoon, Miss Daisy."

"Hi, Jimmy. How's your mom doing?"

He blushed a little deeper, and Ryder realized Daisy had more than a nodding acquaintance with the hand.

"She…she's doing better. The doc gave her new medicine for her arthritis. Winter's always hard on her."

"I guess you can't get away from here much right now to go see her."

"Nope. Not with cows calving day and night. I'm hoping to get back home in April sometime."

As the wind buffeted them more strongly, Ryder said, "We'd better get you inside."

Daisy looked up at him but didn't comment.

Jimmy raised a hand in a wave. "I'll see you

later." His smile was shy, but it was obvious he liked Daisy.

Ryder leaned close to her. "I think he's sweet on you."

"Don't be ridiculous."

"Seems as if you've talked to him before."

"When I visited Leanne over Christmas, he talked about not being able to get home over the holidays. His parents are in Wyoming and he misses them."

Inside the barn, Daisy glanced around, down the aisle lined by stalls on both sides to the clean, scrubbed-out room behind.

"That's the operating room," Ryder explained. "Hopefully they won't need to use it much. I heard Cade say Rand's almost as good with the cows as a vet."

As they walked down the aisle, Daisy spotted a cow licking her young. "Must have just happened," Ryder said with a smile.

Gil Watts came from the room beyond and glanced at Ryder, but his gaze rested on Daisy. "Fifteen minutes ago, while you were still at lunch." His voice was gruff, and Ryder heard again the dislike that tempered any words they exchanged.

"I'm not on watch for another fifteen minutes," Ryder said amiably, "and if you missed lunch, there are sandwiches left at the bunkhouse."

"There's not much here to see," Gil said to Daisy. "It's no place for a woman, especially one in your condition."

Daisy's shoulders straightened and she lifted her chin. "Leanne and Cade thought I might like to see what's happening."

"You've never seen a calf born before?"

"Many times, but not on a spread as large as this."

Gil grunted. "Yeah, well, on a spread as large as this, too many people get underfoot when the calves really start dropping." On that note, he strode down the aisle and out the barn door.

"Don't pay him any mind. He has a chip on his shoulder. You can go wherever you want if you're careful." Ryder found himself looking down at her again, into her soft brown eyes that looked so innocent and vulnerable. He didn't want to take advantage of that vulnerability, he just wanted to know what caused it. She was looking up at him with an expression that told him she wasn't immune to the vibrations that hung between them, whether they were standing out in the cold or in a warm room. What would she do if he kissed her?

He didn't get the chance to find out because she said, "If you have work to do, I can find my own way back."

"Nothing doing. Leanne entrusted you to my care. I'll see you back to the house safely."

They walked in silence for a ways, and Daisy didn't take his arm. He'd thought about what she'd said last night and it had kept him awake, making him consider the women who had passed through his life. One in particular. Sandra Gruber. The daughter of a state senator. A few years ago he'd thought about a future with her. But she'd nixed that idea—because of what he did, because of who he was.

He'd never considered himself a selfish man. He respected women, and when it came to pleasure, he gave as well as took. But when he looked at the broader picture, and that's what Daisy's words had made him do, he saw a pattern. Since Sandra, he hadn't dated a woman more than a week. He also stayed aloof, never giving anything more than the physical. But especially after seeing what Cade had found with Leanne, Ryder realized that his past tendencies could result in a lonely future. Not that he was afraid of being alone, but ever since he'd seen Daisy pregnant…

He'd thought about what it would mean to be a father.

The path to the house was kept shoveled. Though gravel had worked its way up through the snow, there were still some icy spots where the snow had melted in the afternoon sun then frozen at night. As Daisy's foot slipped on one, she grabbed for his arm.

After steadying her, he couldn't resist saying, "Prevention is better than scrambling for safety." He tucked her hand into the crook of his elbow, covering it firmly.

When Daisy was silent, he felt he had to get her to talk, had to get her to reveal how she really felt about this baby. "I suppose a fall could simplify your life."

Stopping, she tugged her hand away from him. "What are you suggesting?"

"An unexpected pregnancy isn't always welcome."

"I love this baby. I have from the moment I found out I was pregnant. For you to suggest I'd want anything to happen to it is insulting." She looked away, then started off ahead of him.

Relieved, he caught up to her and clasped her shoulder. "Daisy, I'm sorry. I just—" He stopped, not wanting to antagonize her or push her further away. "Tell me what it's like. Tell me how you felt when you learned you were carrying a life inside."

She looked almost startled by his request, and then her expression softened and her tone gentled. "It was a shock when I found out. I went to the doctor because I thought I had the flu, but then when the test results came back, I put everything together—the morning sickness, the fatigue, the just feeling really different. My body was preparing and I didn't know it, so I wasn't in sync with it. It's really hard to explain."

He wanted to know more about her and how she felt. "So how did things change after you knew?"

"I was just so much more aware…of everything. I started reading about pregnancy, so with every little change, I knew what was happening. I could feel how my body was preparing. It's such a wonderful experience." She smiled. "Maybe I'll change my mind when I can't see my feet, but I don't think so."

Ryder had known pregnant women who almost resented the invasion of their body and the loss of their figure. But none of that seemed to concern Daisy. She was all-consumed with her child.

"Aren't you afraid of becoming a mother and everything that means?" Fear certainly shot through him when he thought about being a father.

"I've wanted to be a mother all my life. That doesn't mean I'm not a little anxious about it, especially going through the labor part. But after the baby's born, I just can't wait to watch him or her grow, to guide my son or daughter, to form that bond that nothing in the world can break."

He was beginning to realize there was much more to Daisy Harding than he'd ever imagined. He extended his arm to her. "Hold on so you don't slip again. All right?"

She studied him for a few long moments as the wind blew around them. ''All right.''

Trying to not be aware of Ryder's gloved hand covering hers, or his hard strength, or his tall figure beside her, she attempted to put the questions he'd asked out of her mind. It sounded as if he really wanted to know how she felt. That surprised her. She hadn't gotten the impression that he'd asked to make conversation or to trip her up so she'd reveal something she shouldn't. He seemed genuinely interested. But as she'd told him last night, she knew he could focus his attention so that the woman he was talking to felt as if she were the only one in his world. She knew better, even without her sister's warning. Ryder Redstone wasn't trouble to women. He was trouble to their hearts.

Instead of leading her to the front door, he led her to one on the side protected by a small roof and wind blockers. When she looked up at him, she said, ''Thank you for showing me the barn and walking me back.''

''No thanks necessary. Escorting a lady is always a nice break.''

As soon as the words were out of his mouth, he knew it had been the wrong thing to say. That wariness was back in her eyes. ''Look, Daisy, I don't know what you've heard about me—''

''Heard?'' she asked. ''About what a fine rodeo cowboy you are? Or how fast you go through women?''

''You can't believe everything you hear,'' he mumbled.

''So it's not true that you usually take a prize when

you compete in a rodeo, and that's mainly how you earn a living?''

"That's true," he said, proud of it. "The truck I drove here was part of the last prize."

She didn't look impressed. "Is it true you date a different woman every weekend?''

"Where did you hear that?''

"I overheard a couple of the hands talking to Cade one time I visited. They seem to think that's something to emulate.''

Her fancy word told him she looked down her nose at the whole idea. "I move from one place to the next a lot. It's hard to keep long-distance relationships.''

She raised her brows at the word "relationships." "Ryder, your business is your business, and none of mine, but don't try to tell me you're something other than you are."

When Sandra Gruber had laughed at his idea of marriage, of a future, of a family, he'd sworn no woman would ever laugh at him that way again. He wouldn't give one a chance. Daisy wasn't laughing, but she was acting as if her life was so much better than his, as if other men were so much better than he was.

"Don't think I haven't heard that highfalutin tone of judgment before," he growled. "Besides being a calf roper and a man who knows how to have a good time, I'm Cheyenne, too. Someone like you is just too good for someone like me, right? It sure makes me wonder how we ever got it on in the first place. But I guess you weren't looking for a long-term relationship, either. Then again, if you hopped into bed with the next guy who came along, it makes me wonder how different we are, Miss High and Mighty.''

Frustration and anger and the desire to kiss her still burning on his lips, he turned and left her standing at the door.

After he'd strode away a good distance, he glanced over his shoulder, but she wasn't there. She'd gone inside.

He shook his head, chiding himself for his impatience and his lack of finesse. Working a green colt was a hell of a lot easier than dealing with this woman.

Three

The sound of clanging trucks and horse trailers coming up the road outside alerted Daisy to the arrival of the colts. Leanne had gone out to the barn after lunch, assuming Daisy was going to take a nap. But Daisy couldn't get Ryder's expression or his words out of her mind. He'd looked hurt at her attitude, and that was something she'd never expected, although he'd taken her comments much further than she'd ever intended. She didn't look down on him, not by any means. She respected what he did for a living, and she more than respected his Native American heritage. But they were so different, the two of them, and that's what she'd been trying to point out.

Only she hadn't done it very well. Maybe his casual, anything-goes exterior was a facade. If she had hurt him, she needed to apologize.

Daisy put on her coat, earmuffs and gloves, and went outside, taking care as she walked the path to the largest barn. Though she'd grown up on a ranch, she'd never spent much time around the horses. Her father had tried to teach her how to ride early, but when she was only four, the horse she'd been riding had bucked her off and almost stepped on her. After that, she'd stayed away from them. Riding wasn't second nature to her as it was to Leanne. Neither was being around horses. She was afraid of them.

But she needed to see Ryder. Two trailers and the trucks that had pulled them were parked near the rear of the barn. Leanne, Cade, Ryder, Gil and Jimmy were talking to two men Daisy didn't know. She supposed they'd driven the trucks.

As she approached the group, she heard one man saying, "He gave us a hell of a time gettin' in. And he kicked and moved around in there the whole trip. I think you've got trouble."

Cade said to Ryder, "Maybe I chose poorly."

"He just needs to be shown who's boss," Watts said with a smirk. "Give me a day with him."

"Cade, why don't you unload the first one and I'll see about the restless one?" Ryder suggested.

Watts glared at Ryder, but he didn't seem affected by it.

Cade and Leanne went to the first trailer and had no problem untethering the two-year-old and backing him out. Cade let Jimmy lead the Appaloosa into the barn.

Ryder saw Daisy as he came around the trailer, but he avoided her gaze as if he were too busy to be concerned with her. It was obvious she would have to make the first move if she wanted to get back on some kind of polite footing. She thought about returning to the house, but she was curious about how he'd handle this horse.

He opened the small side door close to the front of the trailer and went inside. "Hey, there," he said to the colt, as if he were greeting an old friend. "What's the problem?"

Daisy heard Gil Watts's snort of derision. "If he thinks nice talk's gonna settle that horse, he's loco."

If Ryder heard the man, he gave no indication of

it. Curious, Daisy stepped closer to the open door. Ryder was petting the horse, talking to him in a sooth-ing voice and watching him closely. "So you have a bit of claustrophobia, huh? I can certainly understand that. I like wide-open spaces much better than being cooped up. But you can't have a nice comfortable stall, or any fun, until we get you out of here. So I need your cooperation."

Watts called from the back of the trailer, "Just un-tie him and give him a good shove. Once we get him started, he'll come out."

Ryder answered calmly. "If he puts his head up, let alone rears, he's going to scrape it on the roof. So just stay cool, Watts. I'm not getting him out until he's ready to be let out."

Daisy thought she heard Watts mutter "Crazy In-dian," but she wasn't sure. It was very obvious that Watts's philosophy on handling horses and Ryder's were worlds apart.

She inched closer to the open trailer door.

Ryder's full attention was on the horse. He was chestnut with a white blaze down his nose. Where before she had heard the noise of his hooves restlessly moving on the trailer floor, she now heard nothing but Ryder's voice. It was still low and conversational, as if he were talking to a friend.

Her father had always seen horses as work animals. If they did their job, he fed them and watered them, leaving any other care up to Rand and Leanne. If they didn't do their job, he sold them.

After another few minutes of talking to the horse and stroking him, Ryder called outside, "Open the back...slow. Try not to make a lot of noise."

Watts didn't move from where he was standing,

and Daisy suspected he didn't like taking orders from Ryder. But one of the men who had driven the truck helped Cade to lower the back. Leanne came over to where Daisy watched so she could see, too.

"I'm going to untether you now," Ryder told the colt. "Then we're gonna back out real easy. You and I are going to have to practice getting in and out of here so it doesn't scare you so much."

A few minutes later Ryder backed the horse out of the trailer without any problem at all.

"Well, I'll be damned," the one driver said.

As Ryder held the halter, the colt bumped his shoulder in what looked like a nudge of affection. He rubbed the horse's nose as he looked him over from his blaze to the white spots on his rump. "You made a good choice," he said to Cade. "He'll be fine once he gets used to what's expected of him."

Gil was frowning. "If you don't need me, I've got better things to do."

Cade nodded. "Go ahead. We'll vaccinate those calves when I'm done here. I'll be along in a few minutes."

Daisy followed Ryder into the barn, keeping a safe distance behind the colt. She didn't even think Ryder was aware of her presence until he put the colt in the stall and then looked over at her. "Is there something you wanted?"

His tone held a frost as cold as the weather outside.

"I'd like to…talk to you."

Jimmy had tended to the first colt, and now mumbled, "I'll see ya later," and started walking toward the door.

"Wait a minute, Jimmy," Ryder called. "I thought you wanted to learn how to handle these fellows."

The young man blushed as he looked from Daisy back to Ryder. "I do, but I thought you wanted some privacy."

"Do we need privacy?" Ryder asked Daisy, putting her on the spot.

"I'd prefer it," she returned, standing her ground.

"Get the grooming brush, Jimmy. Daisy and I'll go talk in the tack room. I'm sure it won't take long."

If Ryder wanted to give Daisy the idea that she was being a bother, he was doing a fine job of it. But she supposed she deserved it after what she'd said to him.

Crossing to the tack room, he motioned for her to precede him inside. The smells of leather and saddle soap and hay were strong in the small room. Ryder was wearing a navy quilted vest over a heavy denim work shirt. His Stetson was pulled low on his forehead, his stance was defensive.

"I just wanted to apologize if I said something that...upset you," she began. "I respect your skills with horses and the livestock. Goodness knows, I don't have them. And I wasn't making a judgment. I guess I was just pointing out how different our lives are."

He studied her. "It sounded like a judgment. I know my life's different than most, but that doesn't mean there's something wrong with it."

"I know that."

He bumped up the brim of his hat with his forefinger. "Maybe I overreacted."

"Ryder, about you being Native American—"

"An Indian, you mean?"

"Is that what you prefer?"

He shrugged. "Native American is the politically correct government term."

"Whatever you prefer to use. Being Cheyenne is just part of who you are. Just like it's part of who Cade is. I really don't think about that when I think of you."

"You think of me?" he asked with a sly grin.

She'd tripped up there, that was for sure. Being around him rattled her. "Well…I mean…I couldn't help but think about what happened after the wedding reception."

They stared at each other for a long time, and Daisy wondered if Ryder remembered it in as vivid detail as she did. But that wasn't a question she was about to ask.

After appraising her for long moments, he made a quick change of subject. "Are you skittish around horses?"

Not as skittish as she was around him. "Yes."

His perceptive eyes stayed locked to hers. "Since you grew up on a ranch, something had to happen to make you that way. What was it?"

She felt silly admitting her fears. "Nothing really."

"It was something if it left its mark on you this long."

She stuffed her hands into her pockets, even though they were still gloved. "My dad had bought some new horses. When I was four he put me on one of them. But something scared Buckeye and he reared up, tossing me off. His hooves almost came down on me, but Dad managed to turn him."

Swearing, Ryder mumbled, "No wonder you keep your distance."

"I just had trouble feeling comfortable, feeling

safe, around them after that. It seemed they could sense my fear.''

''They can. Maybe it's time you got over it.''

She patted her belly. ''It's not as if I can ride now, anyway. I don't need to have skills as a horsewoman to teach children.''

''Maybe not, but there's no reason to be scared of them the rest of your life, either.''

''I don't know how to change that.''

''Horses aren't all that different from people. You give them respect, they'll give you respect. There are bad-tempered ones and good-tempered ones, and horses that would give their lives for their rider. Do you want to try to overcome some of that fear?''

''Now?'' Her voice squeaked at the thought of it.

Chuckling, he shook his head. ''Daisy, I'm not gonna put you on one of them. But I could show you how to make a new friend. Are you game?''

''I thought you were busy.''

''I am, but not too busy to get you started. And not too busy to see that fear leave your eyes when you realize you can be as safe with a horse as with another human being.''

In spite of herself, she liked being around Ryder. The excitement that lapped at her whenever she was anywhere near him coupled with a curiosity about him as a man. She felt scared at the idea of getting close to a horse. She'd stayed away from them altogether the past few years. But oddly enough, she trusted Ryder when it came to his ability to keep her safe. ''All right,'' she murmured. ''What do I have to do?''

His slow grin made her insides somersault. ''Follow me,'' he directed as he went back into the barn.

"Get a carrot out of that bucket over there. I'm going to get Jimmy started."

As she picked out a carrot from the bunch in the bucket, she heard Ryder tell Jimmy, "Just take the brush over him slowly. Run your hands over him at the same time. Talk to him and let him get used to you." Ryder showed Jimmy what he wanted him to do, then he came back over to Daisy and crooked a finger at her. He took her down the aisle past Leanne's mare, then stopped in front of a bay quarter horse. "This is Lady Luck. She's mine."

His voice was that low, seductive one that sent shivers up Daisy's spine. She wondered if he'd ever talked about a woman in those terms...and how exciting it would be to be considered his. Then she shook off the notion.

She was a good three feet away from the stall, and he beckoned to her. "C'mon. She isn't coming out, and you're not going in. That way you'll both feel safe."

Feeling as if she needed more courage than she had, Daisy's heart beat fast as she moved toward the horse.

"Give me your empty hand," he said. "But take your glove off first."

Daisy slipped off her glove and jabbed it into her pocket. When she held out her hand, Ryder took it. His skin was hot, his fingers callused, and the feel of him made her breathe faster.

"Now, real slow. We're just going to let her smell your fingers. I promise she won't bite them."

Daisy gazed into his eyes and believed him.

Moving her hand slowly, he held it a few inches from the mare's nose, then let the mare come to them.

Daisy started when she felt the first soft nuzzle, but Ryder held her steady. His chest was behind her shoulder, and she could almost lean back against him. But she knew better. She should know better than to be even this close.

The horse's nuzzling tickled, and Daisy smiled as she realized Ryder was right. Lady Luck had no intention of biting her. It was almost like a handshake. Only Lady's soft breath on top of her hand and Ryder's taut masculine skin under it made the nuzzling a totally sensual experience. Lady lifted her head and stared at them as if asking what was next.

Slipping his hand away from hers, Ryder said, "Just rub her up and down the nose."

As she did so, Lady pushed against Daisy's hand as if she wanted more. Daisy laughed.

"See, she likes it. She likes you."

When Daisy glanced at Ryder, her breath caught. His eyes were almost black, and they seemed to see straight into her soul. Breaking eye contact, she concentrated on Lady and the pleasure she found stroking the animal.

"Now break the carrot in two and hold it out in your palm."

The idea that Lady was going to eat from her palm made her a bit more nervous, and Ryder must have sensed it. "She'll take the carrot and brush over your hand. That's all."

Daisy felt foolish that her fears were so evident to him. Taking a deep breath, she held out her hand. Lady took the first piece of the carrot and made short work of it, then she took the other piece. Stroking her again, Daisy sighed with relief. "That wasn't so bad."

"Nope. You did well for your first lesson. You can come down here and talk to her anytime you want. She listens real well."

Daisy laughed. "And not much back talk, either, I guess."

He smiled. "That depends if *you're* listening or not."

She wasn't sure if he was pulling her leg or serious. The desire to stay here with him and keep talking to him was much too strong. "I'd better get out of your hair so you can get back to work."

"Do you want me to walk you back?"

"No, I'll be fine. But thanks for offering."

They made their way to the barn door, and he opened it for her. When she would have gone out, he caught her arm. "Thanks for saying what you did earlier—about respecting what I do."

His clasp was firm on her arm, and as she looked up at him, her heart pounded. She remembered why she'd gone to bed with him—the thrill of having him look at her as a woman, the excitement of having him want her. "Thanks for introducing me to Lady. Sometime maybe I'll take pleasure in riding." She could stand there forever looking at him, enjoying his company, being thrilled by being with him. He was very close, and as he bent his head, she thought he might kiss her.

"Ryder," Jimmy called, "do you want me to do the other colt?"

Ryder raised his head, and she stepped back.

"I'll see you later," she told him, then started for the house. When she glanced over her shoulder, he was still watching her. She couldn't help but smile.

* * *

That night at supper, Daisy glanced at Ryder often as he sat across the table from her. Collin had left to go back to Garrett's ranch in Elk Springs, and with one less at the table, she was even more aware of Ryder. She passed mashed potatoes and beef and joined in the conversation whenever it rolled around to her. Daisy felt that Ryder was just as aware of her as she was of him.

Midway through dinner Leanne said, "There's a Valentine's Day party at the Hip Hop tomorrow night. Is everybody going?"

Garrett shook his head. "I'll probably stay here and work on the books, but you young folk go and have a good time."

With a forced sigh, Cade said, "Would you believe my wife expects me to dance with her? It could be a long night."

Leanne jabbed him in the ribs. "Keep it up, and I might leave you at home."

Everybody grinned as Cade mumbled, "Over my dead body."

When the phone rang, Leanne hopped up and reached for the extension on the buffet. "Ryder, it's for you," she said, holding it out to him. "A woman." Her tone was slightly disapproving.

Standing, he went to the buffet and took the receiver from Leanne.

Daisy kept on eating, pretending she wasn't interested. But she listened to every word.

"Ryder, here," he said into the receiver. He listened, then responded. "Sure, I remember you, Sue. How could I forget? My dad gave you this number?"

His voice had a laugh and a familiarity in it that Daisy didn't like.

"No, I won't be back in San Antonio for another few weeks at least." His gaze met Daisy's. "Ah…sure. Maybe we can get together when I come back. I'd be glad to show you around the ranch. Okay. A few weeks, then. I'll call when I get back."

Sue was obviously a woman he'd met in San Antonio. And, obviously, a woman he wanted to see again. Daisy felt irrationally hurt. She blamed it on hormones as much as on the cowboy with the sexy smile. It took everything in her for her to try to finish the food on her plate. Each bite tasted like sawdust and she could hardly get it down.

Avoiding Ryder's gaze, she kept silent until Leanne said, "I'll get the dessert and coffee."

No way could she sit there any longer and pretend as if she wanted to socialize or had an appetite. Rising from her chair, she said, "If you'll excuse me, I'm going to turn in early."

Her sister gave her a concerned look. "Are you okay?"

"Fine. I didn't rest this afternoon, and I guess it just caught up. Good night, everyone. I'll see you in the morning."

After a round of good-nights, Ryder's not among them, she left the dining room and went through the living room to the staircase.

But Ryder was beside her before she took the first step. "Is something wrong?" he asked.

"Nothing's wrong."

"About that phone call—" he started.

"You don't have to explain anything to me, Ryder. As we discussed earlier today, our life-styles are very different." So different that her heart ached, and the promise of the afternoon evaporated like a whiff of smoke.

"She was just someone I met before I left Texas."

"And obviously someone you want to see again. Good for you. I'll bet you have women friends at all of your rodeo stops. It must be nice to have such a large selection of...friends."

"There's that tone of voice again," he mumbled. "Don't tell me there's not judgment in it."

She wasn't judging him. She was just reassuring herself that she'd made the right decision in not telling him he was the father. "Maybe what you hear is fatigue, Ryder. I'm tired, and I'm going to bed. Good night." Then she hurried up the steps. She thought she heard him swear, but she wasn't sure. When she glanced over her shoulder, he was gone.

Tears pricked in her eyes, and she wondered why she felt so much more heartache today than she had yesterday. Maybe because this afternoon she'd glimpsed the man beneath the hat, and she'd liked what she'd seen.

But obviously Ryder Redstone wasn't parent material. He was definitely the love-'em-and-leave-'em type, and she promised herself she wouldn't be the one left behind.

"Damnation!"

Ryder brought his truck to an abrupt halt in the slushy, ice-covered parking lot of the Black Boot. He'd been here before with Cade and some of the hands.

As he cut the engine he told himself that Daisy Harding was the most frustrating woman he'd ever met. And that said something, because he'd met a lot.

He shouldn't care what she thought, not when she was lying through her teeth about him not being the father of her baby. He was almost sure of it.

This afternoon he'd thought they'd somehow connected. Jeez... When was the last time he'd even thought of connecting with a woman?

Daisy put him in a tailspin, and he didn't like it—not one bit. Feeling the need to let off some steam, he'd left the ranch after dinner and ended up here.

Climbing out of the truck, he slammed the door, hunched his shoulders against the wind and went inside.

A usual Friday night, the place was full and smoky. In fact, it wasn't much different from the Hitching Post back in Texas. Wooden booths lined three walls and a bar stretched the length of the fourth, with wooden stools that looked as if they'd tip over in a good wind. Tables and straight-backed chairs filled in the rest of the space. The dark-paneled walls were decorated with mounted animal heads. A few mirrors and photographs of the Crazy Mountains gave the place the same appeal as the Hitching Post. It was a safe place for conversation, drinks and a little flirting.

The tables were full, so Ryder slipped onto a bar stool at the middle of the bar, unsnapping his jacket. Since he had to drive back, he either had to stay for a very long while or drink soda.

Loud guffaws came from a booth along the side, and Ryder glanced over. His gaze met the hard stare of Gil Watts, who was sitting across from two of the other hands from the Kincaid ranch. Ryder didn't understand Gil's hostility, but then he'd never understood prejudice and never would.

He'd hardly had time to make a decision on booze

or soda when a woman slipped onto the stool beside him. He could smell her potent perfume without even leaning toward her. She was wearing a tight black sweater with a neckline that dipped to the cleft between her breasts.

"Buy you a drink, cowboy?" she asked in a voice as sultry as she was svelte.

Turning toward her, he liked what he saw. She had blond curly hair that skimmed her shoulders. Her face was a perfect oval with a perfect nose and perfect lips. Suddenly Daisy's face came to mind. It was shaped like a heart, he thought, and her nose turned up slightly at the end. Shaking off the vision, he smiled at the woman beside him. "Sure, you can buy me a drink, then I'll buy you one."

She smiled and extended her hand. "Marita's the name. What do folks call you?"

"Ryder, when I'm not in trouble."

She laughed easily and leaned a little closer. "I can't imagine you ever getting into trouble."

And so it started, he thought, if he wanted it to. But just as suddenly as he'd seen Daisy's face in front of his eyes, he heard the sound of her voice. *I imagine you have women friends at all your rodeo stops.*

Just what was he doing here tonight? Trying to prove her right? Taking out his frustration in one of the ways he knew best? What if he was the father of her child? What did that mean to his life? He'd thought about giving up rodeoing, but he hadn't come up with an adequate replacement. And as far as the women...

He realized that though he thought Marita was pretty—more than pretty—and though she was sitting very close, he didn't feel anticipation or any spark of arousal. That's the way it had been since he'd bedded Daisy Harding. On the other hand, when he got within ten feet of *her,* every part of him practically stood up and saluted.

Nevertheless, Ryder decided a little conversation with this woman wouldn't be a bad diversion. Still, when the bartender came over and Marita looked at Ryder expectantly, he said, "Root beer."

Her brows arched and she laughed, then covered his hand with hers.

He waited for some reaction on his part, but it didn't come. He knew deep down in his gut that it wouldn't.

All because of Daisy Harding.

Four

"Ryder's going to the Hip Hop tonight," Leanne said to Daisy as they cleaned up the breakfast dishes on Saturday morning.

"Is he?" Daisy asked casually, as if she didn't care. She'd heard him come in last night around eleven. Not that she'd listened for his footsteps. She had no idea where he'd gone or with whom he'd spent the evening, and she told herself she didn't care.

"We could go into town, and you could get something new to wear."

"I brought maternity clothes."

"If what you've been wearing is any indication, they're as drab as drab can be. You could use a little brightening up."

Brightening up? Is that all she needed? But then brightening might not be such a bad idea. She'd caught Ryder's attention once. Maybe she could again.

That's silly, she told herself. You're pregnant.

But pregnant or not, she'd still like to give him a good shock. "Maybe you're right. I could get my nails done, buy some makeup. This could be fun."

"Now you're talking," Leanne said with a grin. "Do you know how long it's been since I've been on a good shopping spree?"

*   *   *

Leanne's words were obvious as she stopped at practically every rack in the department store at the mall in Whitehorn. Daisy caught the shopping bug herself as she looked through the maternity dresses, finally selecting three to try on. She would only choose one, though, since she had to watch her money and make her nest egg last. When her parents died and the ranch had been sold, the three of them had inherited a share of the money. Forgetting her inheritance for the moment, she felt the missing—of the ranch near Ox Bow...of her parents. She especially missed her mother right now when there were so many things she could talk to her about.

Their parents had died unexpectedly and tragically in a flash flood on a mountain road. They'd seemed happy their last few years together, and only Daisy had known how troubled their marriage had been at times. Rand and Leanne didn't know what she knew, and they never would. If Daisy hadn't come upon her mother crying that one afternoon, maybe her views about love and marriage and this pregnancy would be altogether different.

Shrugging off the melancholy thoughts, Daisy took the dresses to the dressing room. There was no question about which one looked best. It was soft, red, crushed velvet with long sleeves, a scoop neck and gentle smocking on the front. It was a lovely dress and made her look pretty. Leanne agreed that the dress was flattering. Their next stop was the shoe department where Daisy found a pair of black suede flats. She could always wear her boots to the Hip Hop and then slip into the shoes. They made her feel so much more feminine, and that's the effect she was after tonight.

Since the age of ten, Daisy had worn her hair in a long braid. It was convenient, practical, and she'd seen no reason to change her hairstyle—before now. But today she felt daring. One of the hair salons had an appointment free right before lunch. Leanne and Daisy spent the time before the appointment choosing a lipstick to go with the dress—a burnished red—and a coordinating nail polish. They decided to do each other's nails once they got back to the ranch.

Maybe it was courage, maybe it was the desire to change her life or at least the way she saw herself, but when the hairstylist asked Daisy what she wanted, she simply said she wanted her hair cut in a flattering style and the stylist could do whatever she thought best. Leanne's brows arched, and she sat close by watching as inches came off of Daisy's hair. The end result pleased Daisy immensely. In the braid, her hair had been tamed and subdued. Now it had a chance to have a life of its own. The shoulder-length cut was layered and fluffed around her face in soft waves. She couldn't believe the woman in the mirror staring back at her was her. But it was.

As Daisy readied herself for the party later that evening, she could hear Ryder in the room next to hers. But then he left. She hadn't seen him all day, and he hadn't joined them for supper. Maybe he was avoiding her. As she dabbed blush on her cheeks, she felt more excited than she'd felt in a long time. That excitement had nothing to do with Ryder and everything to do with changes she felt in herself and changes she wanted to make in her life. It was silly, but getting her hair cut had been empowering. Fluffing her hair one last time, she thought, I'm going to have fun tonight. And it didn't matter who was or wasn't there.

She went downstairs when she was ready and found Leanne and Cade waiting for her in the living room.

Cade just gave her a slow smile and said he liked the transformation.

Leanne murmured, "This could be a Valentine's Day to remember."

The Hip Hop's parking lot had been shoveled clear, and it was easy to avoid the few icy spots. When Daisy caught a glimpse of Ryder's truck in the parking lot, her heart started beating faster. Cade held the door for her to precede him and Leanne inside, and Daisy entered a diner packed with people. They were standing by the trays of food on the counter, sitting at the booths and tables, and dancing to the country-western song playing on the jukebox.

Having been here a few times for lunch with Leanne, Daisy had quickly learned the Hip Hop was "the" gathering place in Whitehorn. Anyone could come in here and find out what was going on in the community and in individual lives.

Cade took Daisy's and Leanne's coats and hung them on a rack set up for that purpose by the kitchen door. As Daisy followed Leanne to a booth that was unoccupied, she spotted Ryder at the counter talking to a waitress who had waited on her and Leanne over the Christmas holidays. Her name was Emma Stover. She had reddish-brown hair that was tied back in a ponytail tonight. A few wavy strands escaped and floated around her face. She wore glasses and had a curvy figure that Daisy bet Ryder couldn't help but notice.

As if he sensed Daisy's gaze on him, Ryder glanced over at her. Apparently what he saw made him take a much longer second look. Then, tipping the brim of his Stetson to Daisy to acknowledge her presence, he turned back to Emma.

Daisy's spirits fell momentarily until she reminded herself she hadn't come here tonight because of Ryder, and she'd have a perfectly good time even if he left.

Having a good time didn't mean sitting in a booth with her sister and brother-in-law all evening. She tapped Leanne's shoulder. "I'm going to circulate a little, okay?"

Leanne looked surprised, but grinned. "Sure. We'll keep your seat warm."

As a child and a teenager, Daisy had always preferred spending a lot of time by herself. But in her work she'd learned how to communicate well with others, and especially how to listen. Most people, whether they be kids or parents or friends, just wanted to be listened to.

Seeing Rachel Montgomery whom she'd met over Christmas, Daisy approached her, thinking about all the turmoil the woman had gone through lately. Her sister, Christina, had been murdered up in the mountains. It was discovered that she'd had a baby before she'd died, and Daisy knew that Rachel had hired Jack Henderson to help her find the child.

Providentially, someone had left Rachel's niece on her doorstep, and Rachel had not only found her niece, Alyssa, but the love of her life. The way Rachel and Jack Henderson, married now, looked at each other made Daisy want that kind of bond and that kind of love. She saw it every day with Cade and Leanne, too, so she knew it was possible. But only if two people had the same goals, the same values, the same vision of the future.

When Rachel saw that Daisy was pregnant, she congratulated her, then whispered in her ear, "I'm going to have a baby, too."

Daisy smiled and asked about Alyssa. Rachel adored her niece, and Daisy had enjoyed holding the infant and cooing to her at the Kincaid ranch. She'd known then that she was pregnant, and she'd realized that she loved the feel of having a baby in her arms.

After she spoke with the couple for a short time, Daisy saw Jimmy standing alone by the jukebox. He looked as if he felt out of place, as if he wanted to join in the groups but didn't know how.

Excusing herself from her conversation with Rachel and Jack, she went over to him. "There are some great snacks on the counter."

He smiled shyly. "I know. I'll get some in a little while." After a pause he said, "You sure do look nice tonight."

"Thank you. Would you like to join Cade and Leanne and me at—"

There was a hard, heavy hand on her shoulder, and even before she turned she knew it didn't belong to Ryder. Looking up, she found herself staring into the blue eyes of Gil Watts. He'd slicked his blond hair back from his forehead, and his string tie was crooked. "Would you like to dance, Miss Daisy? A nice slow one is playing."

His invitation was an unexpected surprise, and not

a welcome one. She didn't like his attitude, and she certainly didn't want to dance with him.

Jimmy moved away from them, and before she could find a tactful way to refuse Gil, Ryder was standing beside her with a smile on his face that didn't reach his eyes. "I've claimed all of her dances tonight, Watts. Sorry."

"You two didn't even come in together," Watts growled.

Ryder shrugged. "We decided to meet up here. And now we have."

Gil looked from Ryder to Daisy and then to her rounded belly under the folds of her dress. "Looks as if I'm a little too late. Another time maybe," he said with a nod to Daisy and a dark look at Ryder. He stalked away and stopped at the counter where he picked up a sandwich. But he kept watching them.

"Thank you," Daisy murmured to Ryder.

He didn't respond, but took her in his arms and started guiding her to the music. "I told him we were going to dance, so we'd better dance."

She'd danced with Ryder at Leanne's wedding reception, but it was quite different dancing with him now with her pregnancy between them. Parts of them were pressed together whether they wanted them to be or not, and she felt terribly awkward and uncomfortable.

"What's wrong?" he asked. "Did you want to dance with Watts?"

"Oh, no. I... It's just dancing when I'm pregnant is a lot different from dancing when I wasn't."

Ryder's dark, dark eyes took in everything about her, from her new hairdo to the lipstick on her lips, to her scoop neckline. "You're quite a sight tonight."

"Is that a compliment?"

His voice went low and husky. "Hell, yes, it's a compliment."

Their bodies seemed to be pressed together much too intimately, and heat suffused her cheeks. He must have noticed because he said, "It's pretty stuffy in here. How about we step outside for a little fresh air?"

She certainly was hot, and some cold air might help to clear her head. She needed to be clearheaded whenever she was around Ryder.

Though Ryder didn't bother with his jacket, he made sure Daisy had hers. When he'd first seen Daisy tonight, he'd hardly recognized her. As he'd realized it was her, he'd gotten aroused just looking at her, let alone dancing with her. He'd never intended to dance with her, but when he'd seen Gil Watts making a move toward her, every protective instinct inside him—as well as every jealous one—had raised Cain. When had he ever been jealous because of a woman before?

Never.

It's all because of the pregnancy, he assured himself.

Yeah, sure. It's just the pregnancy.

"Are you sure you don't want your coat?" she asked him as they stepped outside.

"Positive," he growled.

Daisy looked up at the stars, but he could only look at her. "You really do look beautiful tonight."

She faced him, her gaze meeting his. "Beautiful? Or different?"

"Both. What made you do it? Cut your hair, I mean."

"It was time for a change."

He couldn't help reaching out and touching the soft waves that flowed along her cheek. They were silky, and he remembered the night when her hair lay unbound across his pillow. Touching her hair lead to touching her cheek, which was still warm. They seemed suspended in the moment as he stepped closer, and she stayed perfectly still.

"I've wanted to do this since I saw you again," he murmured, bending his head, hoping she wouldn't back away. Because if Daisy kissed him back, if she let her passion loose again, he'd know there was no other man in her life. Daisy was just that kind of woman. This time he wanted to take it slow with her. This time he wanted to take it easy. The first time had been full of hunger and a confusing longing he'd never known, but this time…

His lips brushed over hers slowly, arousing him as he hoped he was arousing her, and he glided his tongue along the seam, teasing, waiting, anticipating. When her arms came up around his neck, he knew he was getting somewhere, and he brushed his lips over hers again, then sensually slid his tongue over her upper lip. Her soft moan was the signal he needed. He slipped into her mouth like the expert he was, but then his expertise vanished. Something about Daisy made him forget who he was, what he was and where he'd been. She was here and now, desire he'd never experienced. As his tongue stroked over hers, creating more heat between them, he told himself to slow down. But his passion didn't understand logic or common sense.

He held her head between his hands, letting her hair fall over his fingers, slide back and forth, tease him as much as her scent as well as everything else did about her. There was no denying the hunger in him, and it seemed her hunger was just as great. She couldn't be involved with anyone else. She couldn't have gone from his bed to someone else's. Not Daisy.

The urgency between them became a tight embrace as their bodies pressed against each other, and he felt the life between them. With a groan he caressed her face, almost feeling more tenderness than desire, yet shaken by a yearning he couldn't seem to appease.

Then suddenly, as fast as she'd fallen into the kiss, she jerked away and wrapped her arms around herself.

"What's wrong?" His hands were shaking, and he just wanted her back in his arms.

"I can't do this." Before he could reach out a hand to clasp her, she turned away from him and almost ran back inside.

He thought about going after her, about taking her someplace dark and quiet and exploring the wild desire between them. But Daisy wouldn't give in to it; she wouldn't give in to him. Because of who he was? Or because of who *she* was? He'd thought her kiss had told him there was no other man and never had been. But maybe that's just what he wanted to believe. There had to be a way to find out the truth.

Maybe he needed to resort to some other method. He'd seen Crystal Cobbs inside. She was Winona Cobbs's niece. For years Winona had been the town's psychic, but no one had really known that Crystal also had the gift until last year when she'd helped one of the sheriff's deputies, Sloan Ravencrest, find Christina Montgomery's body.

Ryder knew that some people looked on Winona and Crystal as odd, but because of his Cheyenne her-

itage, he'd learned to believe in things he couldn't see
or hear. He believed in instincts and visions. Maybe
Crystal could help him out where Daisy was concerned. He'd never met her, but once when he and
Cade had come into the Hip Hop, Cade had pointed
her out to him, mentioning that she and Sloan had
married.

After Ryder wiped Daisy's lipstick from his lips,
he went inside. His gaze went to the booth where
Leanne and Cade were sitting. Daisy was with them,
her back to him, and he knew if he went over there,
she'd scurry away or find an excuse to leave. Instead
he approached Crystal, who was standing near the
kitchen door. As soon as he walked up to her, she
smiled at him. "You're Cade's brother, aren't you?"

"Yes, ma'am. I hope you won't hold that against
me."

She laughed. "Hardly. I'm interested in the Appaloosas he's going to breed. He mentioned you
would train the colts he bought."

"I'm going to start them. He'll take over after
that."

Crystal had elfin features and sparkling green eyes.
Those eyes looked into his now, and he had the feeling she was reading him too well. "You didn't come
over here just to make conversation, did you?"

"No, I didn't." His tone was serious. "I understand you have your aunt's gift, and I need a little
help beyond reason right now."

"I see."

"That's the point, Crystal. What do you see? About
me, I mean. Is there anything I should know? Anything you can tell me?"

"My gift doesn't work that way, Ryder." She clasped his hand gently. "I'm sorry I can't help you."

Ryder realized he'd put Crystal on the spot and asked for the impossible. He'd just have to find the truth using more conventional means.

"I shouldn't have imposed on you like this," he apologized.

"It's okay, Ryder." She released his hand. "At least you believe in what I do...or see. Some people think I'm odd. They see me coming and cross the street so they don't have to pass me."

"It shouldn't be that way."

"But it is. Cade has told me you have a gift with horses. I would imagine some people look askance at that, too."

Gil Watts did. As did trainers who knew no other way but the rough way. "You're right about that," Ryder conceded and then suggested, "Come out to the ranch sometime and watch us. Since Garrett put up the indoor arena, we don't have to wait until spring to get started."

"Maybe I'll do that. Thanks for the invitation."

Glancing toward Daisy, Ryder saw her peek over her shoulder at him. She turned back around quickly.

If she didn't know who Crystal was, and that she was married to Sloan, she'd think he was charming another woman.

Reputations were hell to live up to and hell to live down.

Pulling open the refrigerator door midmorning on Monday, Daisy found the carton of milk and took it out. She'd missed breakfast again, hoping to miss Ryder. She'd managed to stay out of his way over the weekend, only running into him at supper where she usually made an escape before dessert, before he could try to talk to her. Of course, that's even if he wanted to talk to her.

Their kiss the other night had shaken her to her very core. She'd fallen into it with the same sensual abandon that had characterized their coming together before. In the midst of it she'd suddenly wondered why it was happening again—because of the new hairdo, because of the dress, because of the makeup? Was that the kind of woman he wanted?

She'd stopped the kiss because that wasn't the kind of woman she was. She couldn't be a siren who would hold on to him for a lifetime. She doubted if anyone could hold on to Ryder.

And she wouldn't change herself into something she wasn't, not for him...not for any man.

During their kiss Saturday night, she'd realized she was falling in love with Ryder Redstone. Couldn't be. Wouldn't be. She had to stop it right now.

Her thoughts went back fourteen years. She'd come home from school one day and, as always, had gone into the house while Leanne had run to the barn. Rand had been gone by then, working on a ranch elsewhere. Passing her parents' room, Daisy had heard a sound inside. It had sounded like crying. She'd knocked softly on the door, but there hadn't been an answer. She'd pushed it open cautiously, finding her mother sitting on the bed, her cheeks stained with tears, tissues in her hands.

Immediately Daisy had run to her and knelt in front of her. "What's wrong, Mom? What happened?"

"I can't tell you. I can't tell anyone," Carla Harding had said.

But a sob had escaped, and Daisy had put her arms around her mother and held her tight. "Is Rand okay? Is Dad okay?"

"They're fine. It's just…"

Daisy had sat on the bed, then, beside her mother, and taken her hand. "What is it? You can tell me." She'd only been sixteen, but she'd always been mature for her age, more adult than child.

Her mother had looked at her a very long time as tears continued to well in her eyes and roll down her cheeks. "I have to tell someone," she almost whispered. "I can't keep this inside. But you can never, *ever* tell anyone else."

At first Daisy had felt honored that her mother would entrust something so sacred to her. "I promise, Mom. I won't tell anyone. Not anyone."

"Your father's having an affair."

Shock had rippled through Daisy, and she hadn't felt honored anymore, just scared. She'd wanted to yell, "No, it can't be true," but something inside her had kept her quiet. Something inside her had always told her she didn't know her father very well. So she'd done what she always did best. She'd listened.

Her mother had been silent a few minutes, trying to compose herself, then finally she'd started. "Rand wasn't premature, like we've always told everybody. Your father and I had to get married."

Daisy had trembled inside, knowing how hard this was for her mother to tell, knowing that she didn't want to hear it but had no choice.

"He asked me to marry him right away. And I did. But I've always wondered if he loves me. Your father's duty-bound and I'm not sure that's compatible with love. All these years I've hoped…"

"Mom, I'm sure Dad loves you." Daisy hadn't been able to imagine her parents being together all these years and not loving each other. She'd known exactly what kind of relationship she wanted when she got married; she wanted the kind of man who would love her forever and beyond. And she'd thought her parents had had that kind of love.

"This affair is just a symptom of what has always been wrong with our marriage. I've loved your father since the day I met him, but I don't think he can say the same thing. So I don't know what we're going to do."

Though she'd felt terrible for her mother, she'd had so many questions and hadn't known if she should ask them. But finally she asked one. "Has this ever happened before?"

Her mother shook her head. "I don't think so. But I can't know for sure, I guess. Though when I confronted him, he didn't lie. He said it's been going on for about three months."

"What will happen, Mom? Are you and Dad going to get a divorce?"

"I don't know, sweetie. I just don't know."

But her parents hadn't gotten a divorce. They'd gone to the minister at their church for counseling, and somehow they'd put their marriage back together. No one had known that there had ever been anything wrong with it. Except for the minister...and Daisy. She and her mother had never talked about it again, except for a morning about six months later when her mother had come downstairs to make breakfast, smiling. She and Daisy had been alone in the kitchen, and she'd said, "It's going to be all right, Daisy. Everything's going to be all right."

But Daisy had looked on her father differently after that. She'd looked at all men differently and wondered if any of them could be faithful.

Still lost in her thoughts, she took a glass from the upper cupboard and was pouring milk into it when she heard bootfalls—recognizable bootfalls. Quickly she closed the carton of milk and pushed it back into the refrigerator. But she'd only taken a step toward the doorway when Ryder appeared in it.

"Caught you," he said.

"Excuse me?"

"Nope. I won't excuse you this time. We're going to hash something out whether you want to or not."

Five

"We're going to talk about Saturday night," Ryder continued. "I want to know what's going on in your head. And we have to talk about what's going on between us."

"There's nothing going on between us," Daisy maintained.

"The hell there's not! You can't kiss a man like you kissed me Saturday night and then say—"

The ring of the phone interrupted him, and he swore. When it rang again, he muttered, "Isn't anybody else in this house?"

"Not right now," Daisy said calmly. It was unusual to see Ryder ruffled. He was usually so charming and smooth, and acted as if nothing bothered him.

Since he was closest, he scooped up the phone. "Hello?" he barked into it, then a flush settled onto his cheeks. "Oh, hi, Bessie. No, nothing's wrong."

Didn't Ryder get calls from anybody but women? Daisy wanted to know.

He was quiet for a long time while the person on the other end of the line spoke. But then he said, "Sure, I can do that. I don't think that Cade or Rand or anyone else would mind. I'll ask them and get back to you." He looked up at Daisy. "How long will you be at the school? If it's okay with them, I'll drive over to Laughing Horse and meet the boys today."

When he hung up, he looked at Daisy pensively. "How would you like to get off the ranch for a while?"

She liked the ranch, but she found the days were getting long. Leanne wouldn't let her do much of anything because of her pregnancy, and she wasn't used to being idle. Still, she wondered what Ryder had in mind. "That depends."

He sighed and shook his head. "You don't trust anything about me, do you?"

"That's not true. It's just...I don't know you very well, Ryder."

His eyes seemed to darken. "I suppose that's true. How about we remedy that? The lady who called is Bessie Whitecloud. She's a cousin of my mother's. She'd like my help with some of the boys on the Laughing Horse Reservation. Have you ever been there?"

"No. But I've heard Leanne and Cade talking about it. It's almost a self-sustaining community, isn't it?"

"Folks would like to keep it that way, I think— both on the inside and the outside. Bessie's highly involved in the community activities. Most of the time she works at the Trading Post, but she does stints at the day-care center and volunteers as a teacher's aide at the elementary school, too. It looks as if some fifth graders there, a few boys, have been getting into trouble. Detention doesn't seem to be working. She thought if I'd bring them out to the ranch, show them around, give them a few chores to do, it might help them see a life beyond the reservation."

"Do you think she's right?"

He shrugged. "Possibly. It's hard for me to understand since I didn't grow up on one. But I do understand—'' He stopped abruptly.

''What?'' she asked, glimpsing an emotion in his eyes she hadn't seen there before.

He must have decided he didn't want her to see it now, and his expression became shuttered. ''It's not important. Anyway, are you interested in driving out there with me? I'd like to meet these kids and talk to them a bit.''

In spite of herself, she wanted to know more about Ryder. There were more facets to him than she ever imagined. Surely a ride to the reservation would be safe enough. She'd make sure she kept a good foot between them. ''I'd like to go with you. I do get bored staying here.''

A smile slipped onto his lips. ''Okay. I'll go check with Cade and Rand, then meet you outside with the truck.'' At the doorway, he stopped and turned. ''We'll have plenty of time to talk during the ride.''

Then he left, with Daisy feeling uneasy again. Somehow she had to dismiss that kiss. Somehow she had to hide the fact that she thought Ryder Redstone was the most attractive man she'd ever met. Somehow she had to disguise the fact that she was falling in love with him.

Less than fifteen minutes later Daisy sat beside Ryder in his truck, headed toward Laughing Horse. As the miles sped by and Ryder didn't begin conversation, she was surprised. Much too aware of him in the confines of the cab—his broad shoulders, his scent, his jeans-clad leg as he moved his foot from the accelerator to the brake when the car in front of them turned off the main road—she asked, ''Why did your mother's cousin call you?''

His smile was rakish. "Guess she thinks I know something about getting into trouble."

Daisy could imagine Ryder as a wild teenager, getting into all sorts of trouble. "*Do* you know something about it?"

"Not the kind of trouble these boys are into. They've been caught vandalizing property, sneaking a bottle of whiskey into school. It might be pranks now, but Bessie's right. If they keep it up, they'll be headed for bigger trouble." Taking his gaze from the road for a moment, he glanced at her. "Do you know anything about life on a reservation?"

"No. Not really."

"It can be pretty sparse. Unemployment is high, alcoholism is rampant. There have been a lot of good changes on Laughing Horse during the past few years, from what I understand. People who care are making a difference, both Indian and white. But it's hard to undo years of poverty and prejudice."

Ryder told her more about the reservation, the "res" as local folk called it, as he drove there. It was self-sufficient, he said, in that it had a school, a grocery store, churches, the Trading Post, the basics of any small town. The community was tightly knit, and gossip spread as quickly on the res as it did in White-horn.

Curious, Daisy asked lots of questions, and Ryder seemed pleased with her interest. He freely told her whatever she wanted to know. To her surprise it seemed as if only a few minutes had passed before he turned onto the road into the reservation. The streets weren't paved, and gravel mixed with the snow and slush as Ryder's truck easily slogged up the street. He drove up and down a few of them, pointing out Bessie's house before heading for the school.

Ryder parked in the school lot, then came around the truck to help Daisy out. She wondered if he was chivalrous with all the women he dated or just with her because she was pregnant. They walked side by side into the building, and Ryder followed the sign that directed them to the office. The principal was a pretty woman in her thirties with shoulder-length straight black hair and a smile that started in her eyes. She extended her hand to Ryder. "Bessie told me you were coming. I'm Cora Tallbird."

Ryder introduced Daisy. As Daisy shook the woman's hand, Ryder explained, "Daisy's a teacher, too. A reading specialist. I thought she might like to see the school."

Cora nodded ahead of her toward the hall. "I'll show you where Bessie is. She's supervising our trouble-makers. They're washing up the cafeteria floor." As the three of them walked down the hall, Cora turned to Daisy. "A reading specialist? What I wouldn't give to have one of those. Where do you teach?"

"I'm...between positions right now."

"She's staying at the Kincaid ranch for a spell," Ryder interjected.

Cora's face brightened. "Are you looking for a position?" Then she glanced at Daisy's rounded tummy. "Or are you taking time off before the baby's born?"

"What do you have in mind?" Daisy asked.

"I'd love to hire you on a consulting basis. I could bring it up to the Tribal Council and see what they say, if you supply me with your résumé."

"I can easily do that," Daisy assured her. "Working part-time would be terrific right now."

"All right. Either drop off your résumé or mail it to me, and I'll see what I can do."

They reached the end of the hall, and Cora opened one of two double doors leading into a large cafeteria. Four boys were using string mops on the tile floor, and each of them was frowning.

Sitting at one of the tables was a plump, older woman with gray-streaked black hair that was cut short and layered around her face. She stood and came toward them with a smile for Ryder. "You made it."

"Bessie, this is Daisy Harding—Leanne and Rand Harding's sister. I brought her along for a look-see. She's never been on the reservation before."

Bessie tilted her head and studied Ryder, then Daisy. "It's nice to meet you."

Cora said, "If you need anything, let me know. I'm going back to the office. I'm expecting a few calls."

When Cora had left the cafeteria, Bessie nodded to the boys. "There they are."

"I'll go talk to them," Ryder said. "Rand and Cade said to bring them out to the ranch anytime. I was thinking about tomorrow after school. Or is that too soon?"

Bessie shook her head. "Cora can call their parents and get permission. The sooner, the better in my book."

Ryder moved away, then stopped to talk to one of the boys while Bessie turned her attention to Daisy. "Ryder didn't mention he was bringing someone along."

"I was feeling cooped up at the ranch. Leanne will hardly let me lift a finger."

"Are you feeling all right?" Bessie's gaze, too, went to Daisy's stomach.

"Fine, most of the time. I just get tired sometimes."

"Have you known Ryder long?" Bessie asked.

Daisy felt a blush creep into her cheeks. "I met him at Leanne and Cade's wedding. He was the best man and I was the maid of honor."

"I see," Bessie said, her eyes twinkling. "How long will you be staying in the area?"

"I'm not sure yet. I'm a reading teacher, and Miss Tallbird said she might have work for me. If she does, I'll probably stay until the end of the school year."

By now the boys had gathered around Ryder and were listening to what he had to say. The frowns were gone from their faces, and they looked interested.

"He's not only gifted with horses," Bessie observed.

"He's a...complex man," Daisy mused.

"So you see that?"

Anyone who talked to Ryder, and listened, could see that.

"From what I hear," Bessie remarked, "Ryder usually only shows women the side of him he wants them to see."

"He's always very honest with me."

"Mmm," Bessie commented, as if that meant something.

Finished speaking with the boys, Ryder joined Bessie and Daisy again. "I think they're willing to do anything rather than sit in detention or mop this floor. We'll see how they react to mucking out stalls."

Bessie chuckled. "It'll be good for them."

Ryder glanced out the window and saw rain was falling. "Is Joe at the Trading Post?" he asked.

"Not today. He took some of his furniture into town. The store there sold out of all of his pieces." Bessie explained to Daisy, "My husband makes furniture. We sell it at the Trading Post, but also through an outlet in town."

"I'm going to drive Daisy around the reservation before the rain turns to something worse. I wanted to take her out to Jackson Hawk's place, but that can wait until another time."

Bessie gave Ryder a hug. "Thanks for helping out. And make sure you tell your mother hello when you call her."

"Are you reminding me I should?" he asked with a grin.

"It doesn't hurt once in a while."

After goodbyes to Bessie, he and Daisy stopped at the office once more, and Ryder made arrangements with Cora for the boys to come to the ranch.

Back in the truck, he said, "I'll give you the quick tour of the res today. Maybe sometime we can do it in more detail."

As Ryder drove around Laughing Horse, Daisy could see that some of the houses were very well kept and others were run-down. Through the falling rain, she glimpsed the day-care center, a restaurant and the gas station. Then Ryder headed for the main road. As he did, the wind picked up and the drops of rain changed to pinging sleet. The road looked slick already.

Ryder's mouth became a straight line. "We'll see just how good this new truck handles."

"Did you say you won it?"

"In San Diego. There are advantages to being a calf roper," he said with a wink and a grin.

A calf roper who traveled from state to state, rodeo to rodeo, never settling down, Daisy thought.

Ryder concentrated on driving, and Daisy was just as glad. She had no desire to pursue the topic he'd started in the kitchen before Bessie had called.

Suddenly he asked, "Would you really like to teach at the school on the res?"

"Yes."

"You wouldn't feel uncomfortable there?"

"Why would I feel uncomfortable?"

He slanted her a sharp look. "C'mon now, Daisy. The kids and most of the teachers are Cheyenne."

"And that's supposed to make me feel out of place? Listen, Ryder. I've felt out of place most of my life. It wasn't until I started teaching that I found where I fit. Teaching is teaching. Kids are kids. If they approve me to teach in their school, I can do something worthwhile until this baby is born."

Staring straight ahead once more, he turned his full attention back to the highway.

Ryder drove up the road that cut across the ranch and stopped in front of the house, turning off the engine. Before Daisy could ask why, he was out of the truck and around to her door.

When she opened it, Ryder said, "I don't want to take a chance on you falling."

"What does that mean?"

"It means I'm going to carry you."

"You can't, Ryder. I'm…"

"You weigh a lot less than a hay bale. C'mon, trust me."

Without giving her a chance to protest again, he scooped her into his arms, then pushed the truck door closed with his foot. Daisy had no choice but to hold on tightly, her arms around his neck. She remembered too well the feel of his body against hers. Their coats were a barrier between them, but she could still feel his hard strength and the security of being held in his arms. Ryder Redstone was pure male, and that should have made her run in the opposite direction. Instead she wanted to cling to him, and she knew she shouldn't.

Taking deep breaths of the cold, wet air, she told herself rootless cowboys didn't know the first thing about settling down. As far as she knew, Ryder hadn't had a relationship with a woman that lasted longer than it took to bed her. Remembering her mother, how she'd felt as if she'd trapped her husband into marriage, how she'd never known if he really loved her because of it, Daisy stuck by her resolve. She would raise this child alone.

Ryder didn't set her down until he'd opened the door and stepped over the threshold into the foyer. Then he set her on the floor gently, keeping his arm around her. When she looked up at him, she wasn't sure what she saw there, but whatever it was, it fascinated her, just as he did.

His large hand came up alongside her cheek, its warmth caressing her. "You get to me, Daisy," he said in a husky voice.

Her mouth went dry and she knew she was trembling. She just hoped he couldn't feel it. "We're so different, you and I," she murmured.

"That kiss Saturday night wasn't a run-of-the-mill kiss."

"What was it?" she asked softly.

"Special. Too special for you to pretend it didn't happen."

"Ryder, I can't get involved with you. I can't—"

His thumb brushed against her lips, stopping her. "I know you're trying to protect yourself and your child. But I want you to consider something, Daisy. Consider not protecting yourself from me."

Not protect herself from Ryder? That was a concept she couldn't fathom. But before she could manage an adequate response, he brushed his lips across hers, sending all of her thoughts flying. Then he opened the door and stepped back outside into the sleet and rain.

When the door closed, she touched her fingertips to her lips. Ryder's heat was still there, and it burned all the way to her soul.

The sounds from the other prisoners at the state correctional facility for women echoed along the hollowed halls. Lexine Baxter Kincaid thought about her last visit with Audra. It was terrible when a mother had to blackmail her daughter. But blackmail was a bond, and Lexine knew that Audra would do anything she could to escape being arrested as Christina Montgomery's murderer.

Tilting her head back against the cement block wall, she pulled her knees up on the cot. She'd give anything for a good bottle of peroxide to get rid of her dark roots. If Audra wasn't careful with whoever had given her platinum-blond hair that razor cut, more than *her* roots would show. The girl would be a bald scarecrow. She was way too thin.

Lexine shook her head. Apparently Audra hadn't

had the life Lexine had hoped she'd have when she'd
sold her to the man who'd fathered her. Lexine's af-
fairs always seemed to turn out bad, and that one
hadn't been an exception. Her lover and his wife had
wanted a child so desperately they'd paid handsomely
for Audra, and they'd never known there was another
child, Audra's twin. After Lexine had gotten the
money for Audra, she'd deposited Emma in a foster
home. The last she'd heard, that daughter had settled
with a family named Stover. It was ironic that in the
past few months she'd not only heard from Audra,
but Emma, too. Emma had written to her a couple of
weeks ago, requesting to be put on her visitors' list.
The girl hadn't shown up yet, but Lexine knew she
would anyday. Blood was always stronger than doubt.

Thinking back over her life, Lexine felt no remorse
that she'd murdered three men. Her grudge against
the Kincaids still seethed inside her. If she used Audra
right, she could still get her revenge. The Kincaids
had stolen her father's land and, in the process, gained
a sapphire mine that no one knew anything about. Her
life sentence should depress her, but anger went a
long way. If she played her cards right, somehow she
could escape, get that sapphire mine and have her
vengeance on the Kincaids. But she had to keep Audra cooperative, and she had to keep her out of jail.

Lexine heard a guard's footsteps coming down the
hall, and she supposed it was time for kitchen duty.
Damn, what she wouldn't give for a good meal at the
Hip Hop—some elk hash.

The guard was a sober-faced uniformed woman.
Stopping at Lexine's cell, she said, "You have a vis-
itor."

Maybe it was Audra. Maybe she'd realized looking

for that sapphire mine and helping Lexine escape was her only hope.

The guard opened Lexine's cell and pointed down the hall. "Let's go."

The guard followed Lexine through locked doors to the visitors' room. When the guard motioned her inside, Lexine walked down the row of chairs and sat behind the Plexiglas window. The young woman across from her wasn't Audra. She had long, reddish-brown hair with a pretty wave, and she looked as innocent as Audra looked world-shattered. The glasses hid her eyes, but Lexine thought they looked hazel.

Picking up the phone, Lexine waited for an introduction.

Her hands shaking, her palms sweating, Emma Stover picked up the phone on her side of the window. It had taken weeks to get up her nerve to come here. Her search for her birth mother had brought her to Whitehorn. When she'd discovered her mother was in prison for the murder of several men, she'd taken a job as a waitress at the Hip Hop until she could decide what to do. Finally she'd realized that she hadn't come all this way to leave again without meeting this woman. And no matter what happened today, she'd tie up a loose end in her life.

When she picked up the phone, she said simply, "I'm Emma."

It looked as if tears came to Lexine Baxter Kincaid's eyes, and Emma wondered if this woman everyone said had no feelings truly did. They were mother and daughter, after all.

"Emma, honey, you've grown into such a beautiful

young lady. Do you know how many years I've waited for this?''

Waited for this? From what she'd understood, Lexine had simply abandoned her. Still… ''I've been searching for you. I've wanted to meet you all my life.''

''Oh, honey, I wanted that, too. Life's been so tough on me. And men have just treated me awful.''

Lexine was painting herself as the victim, and that certainly wasn't what Emma had heard. But she wanted to try to keep an open mind. ''Tell me what happened. Tell me why you left me all those years ago.''

Lexine's expression seemed to sadden further. ''I was so in love with this man, and when I met him I didn't know he was married. But he was. And when I got pregnant, he abandoned me. What was I to do, Emma? I didn't know how to take care of a baby.''

''But you never came back.''

''I had to find work, and that led me to lots of different places. I couldn't make enough to take care of you.''

''But you never contacted me, never tried to.''

The expression on Lexine's face seemed to change a little. It wasn't quite as remorseful. ''Look, honey, I was just trying to survive. And I knew you were better off without me.'' Her voice had gone into that self-sacrificial note again.

''A child is never better without her mother.''

''Things started happening. I got involved with the wrong people.''

'''Got involved with the wrong people'?'' Emma inquired, afraid to know more yet needing to.

''I almost contacted you once. I thought I'd have

enough money to take care of both of us. But those hateful Kincaids stole it from me."

"What about the men you killed?" Emma asked, getting to the heart of it.

"You're not old enough to understand. Just wait until some man does you wrong. Then you'll feel that rage."

The rage still burning in Lexine's eyes scared Emma. This wasn't a woman with regrets or remorse. "Aren't you sorry at all?"

"Sorry? For trying to get what's mine? I don't think so. And who are you to act as my judge?"

"I'm not acting as your judge. I just want to know why...how you could have done the things everyone says you did."

"You know what, honey? Seems to me you haven't grown up much. Why'd you come here, anyway? Did you think I had something valuable hidden somewhere? Maybe you'll get it as an inheritance after I serve out my life sentence in here? Think again."

"I didn't come because I wanted anything, at least nothing like that. I guess I just wanted the connection girls always have with their mothers. Since you never terminated your rights, the Stovers couldn't adopt me."

"Oh, so now your life is *my* fault? It seems to me, girlie, if you'd put on some makeup and get rid of those glasses, you could attract the kind of man who would make you secure for the rest of your life. Money's a lot handier to have than sentiment."

"I can't believe you're my mother," Emma whispered.

Lexine simply laughed at Emma's distress. "I'm your mother, all right. But it looks to me as if we're nothing alike. I thought maybe we could help each other out. I'd tell you a few secrets, you'd tell me a few of yours.''

"What kind of secrets?''

"The kind that put me in here.'' She leaned a little closer and talked low into the phone. "But I don't think you want to know. I think they'd scare you to death.''

This woman had the devil in her eyes and, being brought up by good people, Emma had been taught to run from evil. And that's exactly what she decided to do. She couldn't help feeling as if she'd lost a dream. Still, losing a dream was better than losing her soul, and if she had anything to do with Lexine Baxter Kincaid, she'd lose her soul. She was sure of it. She couldn't help the tears that came to her eyes, and Lexine saw them.

The woman laughed again. "So you're a baby, too. A few harsh words and you crumble.''

That was all Emma needed. There wasn't even a reason to say goodbye. She hung the phone back on the hook, stood, straightened her shoulders and headed for the door.

Lexine sat back in her chair, looking reflectively at her daughter as she left. This one would be no use to her. Unless…

It was convenient for Emma to show up right now, especially when Audra needed an alibi.

Six

The sun shone brightly Tuesday morning on what was left of the snow as Daisy drove back from the Laughing Horse Reservation after delivering her résumé. Cora had looked it over briefly, then had given her a nod and a big smile and told her she didn't see any problems. She hoped to contact Daisy about the consulting work by Friday. But Daisy's mind wasn't on consulting work as snow-frosted pines and stretches of white pastures sped by.

Rather, she couldn't forget Ryder's lips brushing hers or the warmth of his hand on her cheek. Throughout supper last night, she'd felt so aware of him that she almost thought he'd known every breath she'd taken, as she was aware of his. She had escaped to Cade's den afterward to finish up her résumé.

After turning onto the road leading to the house, she drove to one of the garages and saw a red truck parked by the corral. From his stance, she recognized Ryder as he talked to…a woman. Even from here, Daisy could tell it was the kind of woman she usually avoided. Getting out of her vehicle, she slammed the door and took a more thorough look. Whoever it was was wearing a bright red ski suit, and sunglasses sat on top of her long blond hair. In spite of herself, Daisy was much too curious and found herself walking toward the corral.

"Careful," Ryder said as she came closer. "It's slippery there."

She'd be careful, all right. "I was just at the school at Laughing Horse. Cora said the boys are looking forward to coming out here this afternoon."

Ryder nodded toward the woman beside him. "This is Marita Leaderman. Marita, this is Daisy Harding."

The two women sized each other up. Daisy offered a polite hello, and Marita just nodded.

"Marita wondered if I could train a horse of hers," Ryder explained to Daisy, "but I told her I didn't know how long I was staying."

"Word travels fast," Daisy remarked. "About your horse-training abilities, I mean."

At Ryder's frown, Marita supplied, "Oh, we met at the Black Boot on Friday night. It's not only Ryder's horse-training abilities I admire."

Ryder's face flushed, and Daisy realized that more than talk had probably gone on Friday night. A lot more. Ryder was a charming cowboy who had women at every rodeo stop. She couldn't forget that, no matter how much she trembled when he touched her.

"I see," she said frostily. "Well, I have things to do up in the house."

Ryder called to her as she started to walk away.

But she just kept walking. She knew what was best for her, and it wasn't standing there watching Marita and Ryder flirt. She didn't know how to flirt. She'd never had that type of relationship with a man. Now that she was pregnant, she wasn't about to try to learn.

She let herself into the house and thought no one else was around. But as she hung up her coat, Garrett called from the kitchen, "Hey, Daisy. Want a cup of hot chocolate?"

Hot chocolate and some chitchat with Garrett would be better for her than brooding in her room. "Sure," she called cheerfully, then headed for the kitchen.

Garrett's smile was warm. "I heard you took your résumé out to the res. How did it go?"

"The principal said everything looked good. It will be great to work again. But I don't want to get my hopes up in case the Tribal Council vetoes it."

"Why would they veto you?"

"I'm not Cheyenne, for one thing."

Garrett tilted his head as if assessing her mood. "I don't think that will matter. Is Ryder still down by the corral?"

Daisy sat at the table and tried to make her voice sound casual. "Yep."

Garrett switched on the burner under the teakettle. "You like him, don't you?"

"Sure. Everybody likes Ryder."

"You know, I've seen a lot in my years—seventy plus of them," he added with a grin. "I think Ryder is a man looking for a home."

She swivelled toward him. "You can't be serious."

"Oh, he might not know it yet. But a man who moves around from place to place like he does is looking for something."

"Maybe he's just enjoying the scenery along the way."

His expression serious, Garrett shook his head. "There's a reason he roams. Find out what that is, and you'll find out why he doesn't stay in one place too long."

"It's none of my business."

"Oh, I think it is."

The way Garrett was looking at her, she knew he suspected Ryder was the father of her baby. But she couldn't confide in him about it; she couldn't confide in anyone.

As if he read her thoughts, Garrett assured her, "I've kept a lot of secrets in my lifetime, Daisy. If you ever need to unburden yourself...about anything...all you have to do is tell me you want to talk."

The kindness in Garrett's voice made her throat tighten. Finally she managed, "Thank you, Garrett. But I—"

They both heard the front door slam shut. They both heard the boots on the wood floor as Ryder strode through the foyer and the dining room to the kitchen.

Garrett motioned to the kettle. "That'll take a little while to boil. I have something to see to in the office."

Daisy stood, ready to leave, too. But Ryder unsnapped his jacket and came toward her, determination on his face. "Why did you go running off?"

"I thought three was a crowd."

"Damn it, Daisy. Marita just came out here to—"

"Yes?" Daisy asked expectantly.

"To try to get friendlier, I suppose."

"You mean, you can get friendlier than you were on Friday night?" She kept her voice so sweet it almost made her want to gag.

He closed the distance between them in less time than it took for her to take a breath. "Nothing went on Friday night."

"That's not what *she* said."

"We talked, Daisy. We had a few drinks. That was it."

Her heart felt lighter, but she knew it was only momentary. Until the next woman came along. "You don't owe me any explanations."

Taking hold of her shoulders, he looked down into her eyes. "I haven't slept with another woman since I slept with you."

His words hung in the silence of the kitchen, and Daisy knew she had to tread carefully. "Why not?"

Ryder looked unsettled as well as uncomfortable as he released her. "My life isn't what you think it is. I don't sleep with every woman I meet. I don't sleep with every woman I talk to. Most of the time when I'm doing the circuit, I'm practicing or riding or looking for new horses."

Daisy wasn't exactly sure why he was telling her this. So she wouldn't think badly of him? So she'd tell him he was the father of her baby? Uh-uh. She couldn't let her guard down. She had never trusted a man, probably because of the things her mother had told her. Before she could believe anything Ryder was telling her, she'd have to know a lot more about him and who he was as a man.

The teakettle whistled, and she grasped the sound as an excuse to put some distance between herself and Ryder, to go somewhere where he wasn't. "I have to tell Garrett the water is ready."

Ryder clasped her arm. "You don't believe me, do you?"

"Whether I believe you or not doesn't matter. What you do makes no difference to me."

Then she left the kitchen, biting her tongue. Tears

filled her eyes because *everything* Ryder did mattered to her.

She'd fallen in love with him.

I haven't slept with another woman since I slept with you.

Daisy turned the words over and over in her mind. She'd managed to drink a mug of hot chocolate with Garrett, but then she couldn't sit still any longer. Walking had always been her major form of exercise. It wasn't exciting, but she liked it, and it always helped her clear her head. Today was no exception. She couldn't walk far, and she had to stay out of Ryder's way, but just the trek down to the calving barn would do her good. She loved going in there and seeing the new calves, watching them nurse, noticing how their mothers cared for the babies.

It was almost three-thirty when she reached the small building. Over at the main barn she saw a van and guessed the boys had arrived from Laughing Horse. She was curious about what Ryder was going to have them do, but she wasn't about to go poke her nose in.

Suddenly the door to the calving barn opened and Jimmy almost ran into her. His face turned red as he apologized.

"That's okay. You were in a hurry."

"No, I just…" He had a piece of paper in his hand, and he looked at it with a troubled expression.

"Is there a problem?" Daisy asked.

"Uh…not really. This is just some stuff Gil wants me to get in town tomorrow when Rand drives in for supplies. But I can't read his writing."

"Want me to have a look?"

"Uh…sure."

Jimmy handed the paper to her, and though the printing was small, Daisy could make out every word. "Are you having trouble with your eyes, Jimmy?"

He hesitated, then nodded. "Yeah, I am. Must've stared at the snow and the sun too long."

Cocking her head, she studied him. She'd worked around kids and the printed word and problems with both for the past eight years. "Maybe you should go to the eye doctor and get some glasses."

"Too busy now."

"Jimmy, what are some of the things on this list?"

His face grew red. "That's what I was trying to figure out," he mumbled.

The list included everything from mineral blocks to iodine. She pointed to the third item that was clearly legible. "What's this one?"

Trying to snatch the list from her hand, he said, "It don't matter."

But she clasped his arm. "I think it does, Jimmy. Do you know how to read?"

He looked away from her toward the mountains.

She waited for a few moments, then assured him, "You can tell me, Jimmy. It's okay. I might even be able to help."

"Help?" The word seemed foreign to him, and he shook his head. "No one can help. I was sick a lot in first and second grade. After that my teachers just thought I was stupid and lazy. That's why I quit school. Working seemed a lot more sensible to me than something I'd never be able to do."

"Do you want to learn how to read?"

"Sure I do. Then I could drive. Then I could do lots of stuff I've never done. But it's too late."

How often Daisy had heard those words from teachers frustrated with students, from parents frustrated with their children. "It's never too late, Jimmy. Let me help you while I'm here."

He glanced at the door to the calving barn. "I don't want anybody to know. They'll make fun. They'll say I'm stupid."

"If you don't want anyone to know, they don't have to." Stuffing her hands into her pockets, she thought about how they could work it. "Everyone up at the house goes to bed by nine usually. I can let you in the back, then we can work in that old parlor. Nobody has to know we're there."

"Why do you want to do this, Miss Daisy? Maybe you can't help. Maybe you're wrong and I *am* stupid."

"I know you're not stupid. I want to help you because it's what I do best. I teach students how to read. So at least meet me for one session and let me assess you. What do you say?"

He looked up at the mountains again, then at her. "I should be able to sneak out of the bunkhouse okay, but I want to make sure everybody's asleep. Is ten too late?"

"Ten is fine. You won't even have to rap on the door. I'll be there to let you in."

Jimmy gave her an uncertain smile. "I don't suppose we can start with this list?"

She smiled back. "We might be able to. Bring it along."

His grin was wider than she'd ever seen it. "You better go inside," he chided her. "It's too cold out here for a woman in your condition."

She laughed. "I'll try to remember that. I'll see you

tonight.'' Then she opened the door to the barn and went inside, feeling good that she could help Jimmy, certain that their session would start him on an adventure he'd be glad he undertook.

The soreness in Ryder's shoulder nagged at him, but he ignored it, letting the cold numb it. After the boys from the res had left, he'd helped deliver a calf that was having trouble and wrenched his shoulder in the process. A hot shower ought to take care of it later.

As Ryder took an extra shift checking the calves so he'd miss dinner at the big house, he disregarded the cold and prodded two of the pregnant heifers into the sheltered corral alongside the barn. Daisy was driving him nuts, or maybe it was her opinion of him that was driving him nuts. He was pretty certain by now that that opinion was the reason she wasn't telling him he was the father. He'd almost let it slip today that since he'd bedded her, other women didn't look as good as they used to. They weren't as interesting and they didn't arouse him.

But damn. You don't put that kind of information into a woman's hands. Not the women he'd known, anyway.

He had to find out the truth once and for all about Daisy's baby. Tomorrow he would drive to Sedgemore and do some checking around. Maybe that way he could find out if she'd had any other men in her life, or if he'd been the only one.

Only one. He liked the sound of that.

Voices sounded around the side of the barn. Gil Watts and Rand Harding. Neither man liked him very much, but each for entirely different reasons.

Watts came around the corner of the barn first and stopped under the glare of the floodlight. "We'll take over now."

Rand's expression was a little less stern than it had been since the night Ryder had told him he thought he was the father of Daisy's baby. "Thanks for helping with that calf earlier. Cade said we would have lost it if it hadn't been for you."

Ryder was surprised by Rand's words. "All in a day's work," he mumbled.

Rand nodded toward the big house. "If you hurry, you still might be able to get some dinner."

He was *not* going to hurry. That was the last thing he wanted to do—sit across from Daisy, wondering, wanting her. "I'm going to check on the calf first, then I'll head up."

Gil had moved away by then. But Rand was still standing there, staring at Ryder. "It's a good thing— what you're doing with those boys."

Ryder had heard the story about how Rand had met his wife Suzanne and her brother Mack. The boy had been fourteen then and needed a father figure badly. Rand had supplied that. "I'm trying to do for them what you did for Mack. These are good kids. They just need a positive direction for their energy."

Nodding, Rand agreed. "I know what you mean. How are things going with Daisy?"

There was no point hiding the obvious. "Rocky. But I'm hoping to do something about that."

Again Rand nodded, and Ryder knew Daisy's brother was taking a wait-and-see attitude toward him and the whole situation. "She's quieter than Leanne and me, but she can be just as stubborn."

"Don't I know it," Ryder muttered.

An almost-smile slid across Rand Harding's lips, but then it disappeared. "I better get moving. See you in the morning."

As Ryder checked the calf and her mother, he thought about the strong bonds of caring among Leanne and Rand and Daisy. He'd had those same kind of bonds with Cade and his parents. That was one thing he and Daisy had in common.

When he let himself into the house, he could hear voices in the dining room, but he needed a hot shower before he was fit for anybody's company.

A half hour later the shower hadn't done much for his shoulder. He thought about staying in his room, but the idea of Daisy downstairs drew him as easily as a prize purse at a rodeo. This time as he descended the steps, the voices were coming from the living room, and he distinctly heard Daisy saying, "I can teach you how to crochet. It's easy, really. Then when you and Cade are ready for a family, you'll be prepared."

Cade's deep, male laugh filled the room. "I don't think Leanne is the crocheting type."

As soon as Ryder came into sight, the conversation ceased. An awkwardness came over the room, and he knew it was because Daisy had dropped her head and was concentrating on the yarn and crochet hook in her hand.

"The question is," Ryder said lightly, "whether Leanne would rather crochet or spend her time in the barn."

"I just can't stand being cooped up," Leanne said with a frown.

"Unless it's for a very good reason," her husband

said with a sly smile. When Leanne blushed, Ryder chuckled, but Daisy looked altogether uncomfortable.

Unconsciously, Ryder moved his shoulder, trying to loosen it up.

"Shoulder still bothering you?" Cade asked.

"It'll be fine."

"Cade said you saved a calf. The least you should get for your effort is a good massage." Leanne's smile was broad. "Daisy's great at those."

Daisy's head bobbed up, and Ryder saw the startled look in her eyes.

"Well, you *are*," Leanne reiterated. "Let her work on your shoulder for a little while."

The idea of Daisy's hands on him suddenly made Ryder hot all over. "Oh, that's not necessary."

Cade arched his brows. "We need you in tip-top shape. What do you think, Daisy? Would a massage help a sore shoulder?"

At first Daisy looked as if she wanted to run in the other direction, but then there were sparks of determination in her eyes that made Ryder think, She's going to prove to them that she has no feelings for me and there's no connection between us.

"Sure," she said. "A massage can always help. Take your shirt off."

He couldn't back down from this, either. After all, cowboys weren't afraid of anything, not even a slight, pregnant woman whose hands had done wonderful things to his body once before. Unbuttoning as he walked, he thought, The faster we do this, the better.

"Do you need some lotion?" Leanne asked sweetly.

Ryder could have wrung her neck.

"I have some on my dresser," Daisy answered.

"I'll go get it."

While Leanne was gone, Daisy patted the cushion beside her on the sofa. "Just sit here and face Cade. I'll poke around a bit and see what's sore."

He wished she *would* poke. At least that might not be such a tease. But her poking was more like gentle probing, and the slide of her fingers over his skin aroused him easily. He cleared his throat. "It's really not so bad—" But he winced when she pressed the spot between his neck and his shoulder blade.

"It's this muscle. You should put some ice on it after we're done here."

There were probably other parts of his body that would benefit from ice, too, he thought wryly.

Leanne was back in a few minutes and handed Daisy the bottle of lotion. Cade's smile was smug, and Ryder closed his eyes before he said something he shouldn't. As soon as he smelled the strawberry scent, he braced himself for Daisy's touch. Yet when it came, he wasn't prepared. The slick feel of her fingers was soothing, all right, and a hell of a lot more. He remembered everything about the night they'd made love. He remembered how her fingers had slipped up his chest, how they'd scraped his back when they'd found their rhythm. He swore, realizing that if he let this go on much longer, everyone in the room would know exactly how aroused he was becoming.

He moved away from her hands. "That's great, Daisy. It feels much better." His voice was terser than he'd like, but his restraint was costing him.

"I hardly did anything. Are you sure you want me to stop?"

Hell, no, he didn't want her to stop. That was the

problem. Grabbing the towel that Leanne had brought along with the lotion, he swiped at his shoulder. "Yeah, I want you to stop." He thought he saw a disappointed look in her eyes. Maybe even a slightly hurt look, but he was beyond knowing how to handle her, or what to say or do. Slinging the towel over his shoulder, he held his shirt in front of him and stood. "I think all it needs is a good night's rest. I'll see you all in the morning."

He didn't even wait for their good-nights, but mounted the steps, staring straight ahead of him. Tomorrow he'd have some answers. Then he'd know what to do next.

The calving barn drew Daisy to it again the following afternoon. With the schedule posted inside, she knew when Ryder would be around and when he wouldn't. Today, avoiding Ryder was easy. She'd heard Cade telling Leanne that he'd driven off somewhere, saying only that he'd be back around dinnertime.

Touching him last night had been...

Actually, she'd felt caught between heaven and hell. She'd known if she'd made a fuss about not giving a massage, she'd give Leanne and Cade, as well as Ryder, even more indication that he was the father. So she'd made the best of a bad situation. Seeing him without his shirt had been exciting enough. Caressing his hot, taut skin had been even more thrilling. He'd been fresh from a shower, smelling like soap and man, and she would have loved to have kissed his neck—

Breathing in the cold Montana air, she let out a breath in a big puff of white.

Thank goodness her session with Jimmy last night had gone well. Everyone had turned in, and no one had known she'd slipped downstairs to the back door to let him inside. As she'd expected, she could help him. An assessment had shown her that. He'd looked so hopeful and thankful when she'd told him that she'd given him a hug, and he'd gotten all embarrassed.

Letting herself inside the small barn, she thought it was empty. She liked being here alone, talking to the calves and their mamas. She'd feel silly doing that if anybody was around. Well, maybe not so silly if it was Ryder. After all, he talked to the horses. Two of the stalls were occupied. One of the new calves wasn't even on his feet yet. Daisy watched the mother licking him, wondering how long ago she'd given birth.

Daisy stood there watching for a while before she asked, "How old are you, little fellow?"

Suddenly she felt hands on her shoulders and she almost yelped. Swinging around, she glared at Gil Watts. "You scared the daylights out of me."

"Did I?" he asked in a low voice, still clasping one of her shoulders.

"Yes. Don't you know not to sneak up on a pregnant woman like that?"

"So it would be okay if you weren't pregnant?" he asked in a voice that made her very nervous.

"No, it wouldn't be all right." She tried to move away from him, but his clasp was tight and firm.

"Where're you going?"

Something about this man had made her uneasy from the moment she'd met him. "I'm going back to the house."

"Don't let me interrupt your little conversation."

Gil's hand on her shoulder and his tone were making her afraid. "You aren't. I thought I was alone here. But obviously I'm not."

As she went to move away again, Gil gripped harder. "There's a lot of rumors floating around this place. Maybe pregnant or not, you should think about getting involved with a real man instead of an Indian."

Wrenching away from Gil, Daisy squared her shoulders and quelled her trembling. "Don't ever touch me again."

Gil's eyes narrowed, but he took a step back and raised his hands as if in surrender. "Whatever the lady says. But maybe you should get choosier about the men you...get close to."

With as much dignity as she could muster, she backed away from Gil Watts, then turned and left the barn.

She was shaking, and as she walked up the path to the house, even her footsteps seemed unsteady. She shouldn't be reacting this way. He hadn't done anything to her. He hadn't threatened her. But the tone of his voice had made it seem that way. There was nothing tangible, nothing really untoward that he'd done that she could tell Leanne or Cade about. But if he ever came near her again, she'd scream bloody murder.

As she hung up her coat, she thought about Gil again and the tone of his voice. The whole incident reinforced the idea that she really knew nothing about men.

All of her life, her father, as well as Rand, had protected her. They'd been pretty isolated on the ranch and she'd mostly only come in contact with boys at school. Then when she'd started thinking about them as more than classmates, she'd discovered her mother's secret. It had been a startling revelation that her father could do something so terrible to her mother as have an affair.

All of her life she'd thought she'd known her parents, but after her mother had told her her story, she'd realized that maybe she hadn't known them at all. Feeling unattractive as a teenager, associating mostly with girls and her sister, she hadn't dated. Even in college she hadn't sought male companionship. Now she realized that maybe she'd been fearful of it.

So what in good heavens had happened with Ryder?

She'd probably never be sure. It didn't really matter now. Only her child did. Whether she'd had too much to drink or had felt pretty or had fallen under Ryder's spell or had decided having a baby at any cost was worth whatever she had to do, didn't matter, either. But her unborn child's future did.

Her hands were shaking, and she went to the kitchen to make herself a cup of tea. There were no sounds in the house, and it seemed empty. But the idea of sitting and having a cup of tea in the silence didn't appeal to her. She needed something to do, something that would shake off the feel of Gil Watts's hand on her shoulder, something that would get his voice out of her head.

One thing her sister hated doing was cleaning. Daisy had noticed a thin film of dust collecting on the furniture. She imagined the place could use a good housecleaning. Cleaning always made her feel as if she were putting herself in order. Maybe the physical activity would help. Maybe she'd forget about the past half hour.

But a little voice in her head told her forgetting was never as easy as it sounded. As she went to the utility closet in the kitchen for a dust cloth and turned the knob, she saw that her hand was still shaking.

Seven

The town of Sedgemore was larger than Whitehorn, but not so different. It had its main street with shops, banks and insurance offices, a few restaurants and diners, side streets that led like spokes to developments that had sprung up near schools or shopping centers. Stopping at a pay phone at a gas station, Ryder found Daisy listed in the phone directory. The clerk working at the convenience store gave Ryder directions to the address.

She lived in a home in the older section of town. Her apartment was listed as 704-B, so he figured it was either in the back or upstairs. There weren't many cars on the tree-lined street, and he parked between piles of snow in front of a house covered with beige siding and hung with brown shutters. A narrow porch wrapped it from front to side, and there was a walk alongside it that led to the back. Before he pulled his old-friend charade, he'd take a good look around.

He found 704-B at the back of the house. There was a wooden door with a glass pane and curtains swagged across it. Peering inside, he could see a flight of steps. It was an upstairs apartment, all right. Now the question was whether or not Daisy's downstairs neighbor was friendly. There was only one way to find out.

Walking on the snow-melted walk to the front

porch again, Ryder went up the two steps, then knocked at the front door.

A few seconds later an elderly woman opened it. "Can I help you?" she asked. Her hair was mostly white and she wore it in a bun at her neck.

He produced his best smile. "I'm sorry to bother you, ma'am, but I'm looking for Daisy Harding."

The woman peered at him over her wire-rimmed spectacles. "She's not here right now."

"Do you know when she'll be back? I'm an old friend and I'd hate to miss her."

The woman tilted her head and studied him. "I've never seen you around here before."

"That's because I'm visiting the area from Texas."

"You've come a long way," the woman said.

"That's why I don't want to miss her. Do you know when she'll be back?"

"Not exactly. A couple of weeks, maybe."

"Oh, I'll be long gone by then," he mused regretfully. "Tell me, is she doing okay? I worry about her. She told me she was pregnant."

The woman seemed to relax at that, as if she finally believed he was an old friend. "She went to stay with her sister in Whitehorn for a spell. I think she's doing okay."

"Did her boyfriend go with her?"

A blank look crossed the woman's face. "Her boyfriend?"

"Yes, the baby's father. Did he go with her to Whitehorn?"

"I've never seen the baby's father."

"You mean, he's not hanging around here every night, taking care of her?"

"Daisy doesn't talk about him, and I'm not one of those nosey landladies. I stay out of her business."

"I'll bet she's grateful for that."

"She's been a fine tenant for eight years."

"I bet you don't even know she's up there. Daisy's so quiet."

"That she is. No parties or shenanigans for that girl. That's why I was so surprised when…"

"When?" Ryder prompted.

The woman looked chagrined that he'd caught her in a bit of gossip. "When I saw she was pregnant. But she seemed happy about it, not at all disturbed. So I figured she'd be marrying the father soon."

"Do you know his name?" Ryder asked.

"No, I don't. Do you?"

"No, ma'am, I don't, but Daisy told me he's a fine man."

"That's more than she's told anyone around here. We figure she's just a bit ashamed for getting caught without a wedding ring. But if he's a fine man like you say, he'll take care of that right quick."

"Well, I guess I'll try to get in touch with Daisy in Whitehorn. I do thank you for your help. Can you tell me where the best place is to eat close by? Maybe someplace where Daisy gets suppers out once in a while."

"She likes that little diner over on Oak. You can't miss it. They've got a bright red-and-white sign up."

"Thank you again for all your help. You have a good day now."

Before the woman could ask him any questions, Ryder headed down the steps, straight for his truck. He almost felt like whistling. It seemed no men had been buzzing around Daisy, and he'd bet his best pair of boots that when she ate at that diner, she ate alone.

As he tried the blue plate special at the Oak Street Diner, he talked with a waitress who knew Daisy from his description. She was talkative and revealed that Daisy came in a couple of times a week, always by herself. She'd never seen her with a man.

Ryder was feeling more and more confident.

On the hour-long drive back to Whitehorn, he did whistle. He even sang a little. Then the radio kept him company as he thought about the best way to convince Daisy to trust him. Because that was what this was going to take—gaining her trust.

When Ryder returned to the ranch, he parked the truck in one of the garages, then went to the house. He wasn't sure what he was going to say to Daisy. He'd just have to let his gut lead him.

As he stepped into the entranceway, he heard a whirring sound. After he hung up his hat and jacket, he followed the noise and found Daisy vigorously using a sweeper attachment on the sofa.

At first he wanted to run over and grab it from her. She shouldn't be pulling a sweeper around. But his better sense told him she wouldn't like interference. So instead he watched her a few minutes. She was dressed in denim slacks and a deep purple top, totally intent on what she was doing. His gaze passed over the slenderness of her body and the roundness of her tummy. As she bent to lift a sofa cushion, her silky hair glided along her cheek. He liked it shorter, flowing freely around her face. She had such a pretty face.

All of a sudden Daisy grabbed for the arm of the sofa, as if to steady herself. The sweeper hose and nozzle fell from her hand to the floor.

Without a moment's hesitation Ryder crossed to her, curved his arm around her waist and helped her sit on the sofa. With his foot he clicked off the sweeper. She was pale and beads of perspiration stood on her brow.

"What's the matter, Daisy?"

"Just a little…dizzy."

"Put your head down between your legs."

When she didn't do it right away, he urged her, "C'mon. It'll make you feel better."

When she did as he directed, he took one of her hands. It was clammy, and he was scared that something was really wrong. "Who's your doctor? Let me call him."

She kept her head down, but shook it. "Uh-uh. This will pass. It's happened before."

Her voice was a bit muffled and didn't make him feel any better. "Don't move," he warned. "I'll get you a glass of water."

Not only did he fetch a glass of water, but he found a washcloth, held it under the spigot and wrung it out. Then he hurried back to her. Sitting beside her, he moved her hair to the side of her neck and held the cloth there. She started, but didn't sit up.

After a few minutes when all he could hear was the pounding of his heart, he asked, "How are we doing?"

Raising her head, her hand went to the washcloth on the back of her neck. But he was still holding it, and her fingers brushed over his. "Better. I guess I just…overexerted myself."

He didn't like the troubled look in her eyes. "What's the matter, Daisy? Is it the baby?"

She shook her head. "No. No, the baby's fine. I just tried to do too much too fast, I guess."

He stood and ordered, "Swing your legs up on the sofa."

"Ryder, I'm fine. Really."

"Swing your legs up, Daisy. I'm not letting you leave here until you've rested awhile." He handed her the glass of water.

He really knew something was wrong when instead of arguing with him, she dropped the cloth onto the floor, did as he'd ordered and sipped the water. There was still a look in her eyes...

"What made you decide to act like a cleaning service?"

As she set the glass down on the coffee table, she avoided his gaze. "The place needed it."

Wanting to take her in his arms and hold her, he restrained the urge and, instead, lowered himself to the sofa, beside her hip. "If you're bored, I'm sure Cade can put you to work on the computer."

"I'm not bored." She kept her eyes cast down at her hands in her lap.

Putting a finger under her chin, he gave a little nudge until her gaze met his, and then he was surprised when her brown eyes became shiny, and she bit her lower lip.

"Daisy, what's wrong?"

"I didn't want to tell anyone."

"Tell anyone, what?"

"I went out to see the calves, and I thought I was alone there."

"I heard rumors you like to talk to them," Ryder said with a gentle smile. She blushed and he was relieved that, at least, color had come back into her cheeks. "So you were talking to the calves... Then what?" he urged, his voice husky.

"Gil Watts was there."

Ryder's heart started pounding hard again. "What did he do to you?"

She quickly shook her head. "He didn't do anything, Ryder. That's why I wasn't going to say anything."

"Then what has you so upset?"

"I'm not upset. I'm—"

"Yes, you are. I can tell." Taking her hands in his, he held them. "What happened down there? Did he touch you?"

"No! I mean he just put his hands on my shoulders. It was the tone of his voice."

Ryder knew Gil Watts could make a statement with an inflection. "What did he say to you?"

She just shook her head again.

"Damn it, Daisy! I'll go wring it out of him if you don't tell me."

"No. Don't do that. That's what I don't want."

"Then what did he say?"

"He insinuated...he said..."

Ryder squeezed her hands tighter.

"He just said I should find out what it's like to be with a real man."

"I think you're leaving something out."

"If I am, it's not important."

"The hell it's not! Tell me what he said."

Still she hesitated.

"I can guess," he muttered. "Some remark about me being Cheyenne."

When she gave a slight nod, Ryder swore viciously. "Watts is a prejudiced S.O.B. I've met the likes of him before. And he's not going to get away with scaring you.'' Ryder pushed himself to his feet, ready to confront Watts and deck the man if he had to.

But Daisy grabbed for his hand. ''Don't. Please, Ryder. Don't make something of this. I really just want to forget about it. I don't want to make trouble, not for you or Cade or anyone.''

''I'll talk to Rand, and he'll fire him.''

''No,'' she said loudly. ''Don't you see? That would be like stooping to his level and only make him think worse of all of us. Please, just let it go.''

Let it go. How many times had Ryder heard that? That was his parents' philosophy, too. But all of it built up inside a man over the years. Still, looking into Daisy's soft brown eyes, seeing the paleness on her face, he wanted to abide by her wishes, too. ''I won't ask Rand to fire him.''

''Ryder…''

Something in his voice must have tipped her off. He stroked the top of her hand. ''Trust me on this, Daisy. I won't make a big stink. But that doesn't mean I'm not going to say something to Watts.''

''I don't want you to end up in a fight.''

''Afraid I'll hurt something important?'' he asked, trying to take a lighter tone.

With a roll of her eyes, she blew out a breath and made a move to get up from the sofa.

''Where do you think you're going?'' He didn't budge, and he wasn't going to.

''I have to finish what I was doing, and then put everything away.''

''I think you need to use some common sense. I'll put everything away. Whatever you didn't finish can wait until another time. C'mon, I'll take you upstairs."

"You won't take me anywhere. I'm perfectly capable of getting to my room."

"You're perfectly capable of too many things," he muttered as he stood, knowing a few words weren't going to stop her. He watched her as she got to her feet, and to him, she still seemed a little shaky. "Can I get you something? I mean, I'll bring it up if you want me to."

When she tilted her head, she looked at him pensively. "A glass of milk and one of those biscuits we had for breakfast would be great."

A grin spread across his face. If she was hungry, then she'd be okay. "A biscuit and milk it is."

She moved away from him then, and he wanted to catch her, pull her into his arms. He didn't understand the yearning to hold Daisy, any more than he understood the mysterious feelings that churned inside him when he thought about being a father. But he did know he'd move heaven and earth to protect her and their unborn child.

He watched her carefully as she climbed the stairs. She seemed steady on her feet, but he wanted to make sure. When she reached the hall upstairs, he went to the kitchen for the milk and biscuit.

A few minutes later he pushed open the door to her room. She was standing at the window, looking out at the landscape.

"A quarter for your thoughts," he teased as he set the dish and glass on her dresser.

She smiled. "Whatever happened to a penny?"

"Inflation."

She laughed, then became serious again. "I was

just thinking about when we lived on a ranch when we were kids. I didn't spend much time around the animals, but I loved the feel of being there. I could walk for miles and still be at home. Do you know what I mean?''

''Sure do. Your world filled up your life and when it got too tough in other places, you could run back there.''

''Something like that. Things changed when I was a teenager—'' She stopped and looked away.

Coming up beside her, he turned her toward him. ''What things changed?''

''It's not important.''

''Don't do that, Daisy.''

She looked surprised. ''Do what?''

''You often make light of what you're thinking or what you're feeling.''

''Sometimes it's better to make light of it than to dwell on it.''

After thinking about that for a few moments he offered, ''You don't have to dwell on it, but I do think you have to face it.''

Her shoulders lifted in a small shrug. ''Maybe.'' Glancing at the dresser, she said, ''Thanks for bringing that up. And thanks for being here this afternoon. It helped. I shouldn't have gotten so upset.''

He gave her a scolding look. ''You had every right to get upset.''

The way she was looking at him, he couldn't help but put his arms around her and pull her to him. Unexpectedly, she didn't step back, and he felt pleased. She was so damned independent. But this afternoon had shaken her, and she'd needed to lean on someone. He liked the fact that she'd leaned on him. Desire coursed through his body, but he knew he couldn't give in to it this time. This wasn't that kind of moment. After just holding her for a short while, he leaned back slightly and placed a kiss on her forehead.

She looked up at him, startled, but he just smiled at her. ''You eat your snack and then rest. If you need anything, call over to the barn. Somebody can come get me.''

Pulling away from him, she stepped back. ''I'll be fine.''

Daisy Harding's strength was as much a part of her as her quiet ways. She was back to herself again, and he realized he was a little sorry, but also glad.

Fifteen minutes later Ryder headed toward the maintenance shed. One of the hands told him Gil Watts was there, working on a truck. When he saw Watts standing by the raised hood, fury filled him for the fear the man had put into Daisy. But he clamped it down, warning himself that, above all, he had to stay calm. Daisy would be upset if he started something, and he didn't want to upset her any more than she already was.

Watts lifted his head from looking into the engine. Seeing Ryder, he grimaced. ''Something wrong?''

''You know damned well something's wrong. You ever go near Daisy Harding again, you so much as put a finger on her, and you won't remember your name, let alone where you came from. Understand?''

The expression on Gil Watts's face told Ryder the man understood, but he didn't like it. ''She's not your property.''

''That's true. Daisy's not anyone's property. But I

won't see her hurt, and I won't see her upset. So you stay away from her.''

''What makes you think the little lady doesn't like my attention?'' Watts goaded.

''She told me.'' Ryder's voice was even and low, warning Watts not to make an issue of this, because he wouldn't be pushed.

With an insolent shrug, Watts mumbled, ''Fine. I'll stay away from her.''

Relieved, Ryder turned away.

''But, Redstone, that doesn't mean I'm doing it because you told me to.''

Ryder knew if he continued this, they'd end up in a fist fight, so he slammed the door of the shed and walked into the cold afternoon, needing to take a deep breath, needing to let tolerance take the place of anger.

After a late shift checking the heifers that evening, Ryder made himself a sandwich in the kitchen, listening to the silence in the rest of the house. It was almost ten, and he wanted to check on Daisy to make sure she was okay, but he didn't want to disturb her if she was sleeping.

He'd gone upstairs to his room and stripped down to his jeans when he heard the soft creak of the floor in Daisy's room. Maybe she was still awake. When he opened his door, he saw her scurrying down the hallway with something in her arms. He hadn't even heard her door open. Had she done it quietly on purpose?

Maybe she just needed a glass of milk to help her fall asleep.

But what was she carrying?

Deciding answers were better than wasting time asking questions, Ryder followed her. She didn't turn toward the kitchen, but rather went through the living room to the back hall. There was another sitting room down there, as well as guest bedrooms. He passed a few glass cases where artifacts such as pottery bowls, ceremonial pipes, blankets and a buffalo headdress were displayed. Garrett had explained to him they were from many tribes and had been there for years. But right now Ryder was more concerned with what Daisy was doing at the back door than he was about Kincaid treasures.

His bare feet helped him move silently, and he came up behind her just as she was letting Jimmy Mason in the door, saying, "Coast is clear, Jimmy."

"The coast is clear for what?" Ryder asked suspiciously.

Daisy's hand went across her breast, and she gave a small yelp. "Don't sneak up on me like that!" she chided him.

"Looks to me like you're the one doing the sneaking. What's going on?"

Jimmy couldn't seem to decide whether to come in or go out, and Ryder wanted to get to the bottom of this late-night rendezvous. "C'mon in, Jimmy. You're letting in cold air."

Daisy put her fingers to her lips. "Sh-h-h. We don't want anybody to know."

"And just what is there to know? Are you two having an affair?"

Jimmy's face turned beet red, but Daisy just looked angry. "Your mind would go there."

So they were back to that, were they? "My mind goes where it's led."

Close to her now, he saw the newspaper and magazine, as well as the box that looked like some kind of cards kids might use. Suddenly it hit him. He looked from one of them to the other. "Is this a tutoring session?"

Daisy looked at Jimmy. "I know he won't tell anyone."

The young man shifted on his feet, his hat in his hands. "Daisy's teaching me how to read."

"I see," Ryder said slowly. "How long has this been going on?"

"This is only our second session," Daisy answered. "But Jimmy doesn't want anyone else to know."

"I didn't know he couldn't read." To Jimmy he said, "You've done a good job of covering up."

"All my life," Jimmy mumbled.

"Your secret's safe with me." Ryder took the stack of things from Daisy's arm and handed them to the young man. "Go ahead in awhile. I'd like to talk to Daisy for a few minutes."

Jimmy's gaze found Daisy's as if checking to see if that's what she wanted, and she nodded. Brushing by Ryder, he went into the small sitting room.

Daisy was wearing a white long-sleeved sweater that was fuzzy and soft, along with stretchy pants that fit the curve of her calves beautifully. "Did he ask for your help?" Ryder asked her.

"I discovered by accident that he couldn't read. I told him I could show him a whole other world if he'd let me teach him."

Ryder was beginning to believe Daisy could show *him* a whole other world, too.

Her gaze dropped to his bare chest and he felt his

blood get hot. When her eyes came back up to his, there was something in the air. There was always something in the air when they were anywhere near each other.

"Are you feeling okay?" His voice was deep, and he wondered how one woman could affect so many things about him.

Her smile was sweet. "I'm fine."

"No more dizziness?"

"No. I think between stooping over and what happened, I just got a little light-headed. I'm going to check in with Leanne's doctor as soon as I can get an appointment just to make sure."

He took a step closer to her until his belt was brushing her tummy. "I spoke to Watts. If he knows what's good for him, he won't bother you again."

His heart seemed to beat in tandem with hers as she studied him, then murmured, "Thank you."

He'd missed her tonight. He'd not only wanted to see how she was, he'd wanted to be with her. He didn't understand it, any more than he understood the need to have her in his arms, the need to have his lips on hers...

The thought became action. She felt so good. And when he bent his head to kiss her, he knew she wasn't going to pull away. "Daisy," he breathed a moment before his lips caught hers. Their lips sealed to each other for a few moments, but then Ryder wanted much more. His tongue breached their seam, and she welcomed him.

He'd so desperately wanted to touch her again since that first time. Holding her head steady with one hand, he thrust his tongue into her mouth and stroked against hers until she moaned softly. As if it had a mind of its own, his other hand went to her breast. The sweater tickled his fingers as her small breast filled his palm. It was fuller than before. He noticed that right away. She moaned again as he gently stroked her, and he became fully aroused. Desire burned fiery hot, and all he could think about was taking her someplace private. His thumb grazed her nipple, and she reacted with abandon, lacing her fingers in his hair.

Breaking the kiss, he still held her in his hand, trailing more kisses along her cheek, down her neck.

"Ryder."

She sounded as breathless as he felt. Much more of this, and they'd be on the floor.

With an audience.

Reason finally overcame desire as he remembered Jimmy was waiting for Daisy in the room a few feet away. He shouldn't have started this here.

But something about this woman made him forget his common sense.

Slowly he raised his hand from her breast and cupped her face between his palms. "You're so sweet. Do you know exactly what I'd like to do with you?"

She blushed, and as she realized how far they'd gone, she took a step back. "I'm pregnant, Ryder. This can't happen."

"You're pregnant because this happened."

"No. I mean…you…me…we can't do this."

Suspecting that in the throes of the kiss she'd wanted the passion as much as he had, he replied, "We want each other, Daisy, whether you're ready to admit it or not. And pregnant women can have just as much fun as non-pregnant women. At least, that's what I've heard. So don't use it as an excuse. And don't deny what happens when we kiss and touch. Think about it. Think about us. Think about trusting me with the truth.''

Her eyes grew very large, and as he stepped away from her, her lower lip trembled.

"You've had a long day," he reminded her. "Why don't you keep this session short?''

Then, tempted to take her in his arms again and start the whole thing over, he walked past the artifacts and into the living room.

Daisy's head was spinning, and she knew she had to compose herself before she could even talk to Jimmy, let alone teach him. Ryder always made her world turn upside down. How could she have acted like that with Jimmy right there in the parlor? Shaking her head, she dropped her arms to her sides and took several deep breaths. Her cheeks were still hot, but there wasn't anything she could do about that. Crossing to the parlor, she went inside.

Jimmy looked up at her. "You really don't think he'll say anything?''

Daisy was glad Jimmy hadn't commented on how long she'd been. But then, he wouldn't. He was polite to a fault. "He won't. He knows how important this is.''

Sitting on the elaborately carved love seat, she took the box of flashcards from the marble-topped table. "We're going to start with sounds," she told him, glad her cheeks were cooling down, hoping she could forget about Ryder, at least for the time being.

Eight

The following morning, Daisy went to see Leanne's doctor. After calling her physician in Sedgemore and checking her over, he decided her pregnancy was progressing nicely and told her she had nothing to be concerned about. Relieved, she did her best to forget about yesterday.

Later that afternoon, as she was gathering more materials to use with Jimmy—a horse magazine she'd found in Cade's study, the television listings—the phone rang. She picked it up. "Kincaid ranch."

"Daisy? Is that you?"

Her landlady's voice was soft with a high inflection that Daisy recognized immediately. Hannah Bowman was watering Daisy's plants and generally watching over her apartment for her. "It's me, Hannah. Is something wrong?"

"I'm not sure. There was a man here, looking for you."

A man? Must have been a salesman—maybe the insurance agent who was trying to convince her to invest for the future. But he usually called for an appointment.

"Nice-looking cowboy," Hannah went on. "Right friendly, too. He said he was a friend of yours."

Puzzled now, at a loss as to who it could be, Daisy asked, "What did he want?"

"Just said he hadn't seen you for a while. He seemed disappointed he missed you and asked when you'd be coming back. Said he's been livin' in Texas."

The words "cowboy" and "Texas" alerted her to a possibility she didn't like. "Did he ask any other questions?"

"Just wanted to know if you're doing okay. Said he knew you were pregnant. When I told him you were staying with Leanne, he asked if your boyfriend went along with you. I told him I've never met your fella."

Ryder. It had to be. First annoyance, then anger, rippled through Daisy. How dare he snoop around behind her back? How dare he poke into her life? "Hannah, did he have dark brown hair, really dark eyes and a smile that—that made you want to answer all his questions?"

"You're right about the hair and eyes, and yes, he had a nice smile. Is he an old friend?"

"I wouldn't exactly say that."

"What should I tell him if he comes back?"

"He won't be back, Hannah. I'll take care of it. But thanks for calling me. How are you doing?"

"Pretty good. My blood pressure's been behavin'."

After speaking with Hannah for a while longer, Daisy thanked her again for calling, then hung up.

When she thought about Ryder investigating her like some private detective, she began fuming all over again. He wasn't going to get away with it.

After calling down to the barn and finding out from Leanne that Ryder was in the training arena with the colts, Daisy headed that way without a second thought. Inside, she saw a wire mesh pen set up within the bigger arena. Ryder was inside with a colt; Jimmy was watching.

When Ryder saw her, he smiled. But she was having none of that. Going over to the pen, she asked, "Can I talk to you?"

His smile slipped away, and he handed a coiled rope to Jimmy. "Just do what I've been doing with him. You'll be fine. I won't be long."

After Jimmy went inside and closed the gate behind him, Ryder walked with Daisy over to the line of holding stalls. The moment they stopped, she turned to him. "How dare you?"

His expression took on one of the "uh-oh" kinds of looks, but he didn't try to charm her with one of his smiles. "How dare I what?" he asked in a low voice.

"Did you go to Sedgemore?"

"Yes, I did."

"Why?"

"To find out the truth."

"You had no right to snoop around and ask my landlady questions. No right at all," she said in a vehemently low voice that shook.

"If I'm the father of this child, I have plenty of rights."

Tears came to her eyes when she thought about what she wanted, what she wished for and the reality of the way things really were. "I've told you the father of this baby is my business, and my business only. Stay out of my life, Ryder. I don't want you in it."

"That's not the way it seemed last night." His voice held an edge of anger of his own.

"You took me off guard last night."

"Just like the first time? Stop denying that you want me as much as I want you. Because denying it isn't going to make the chemistry go away."

"Chemistry is the last thing I need in my life right now." Before she broke into tears in front of him, she ran for the door.

He caught up to her outside, but Bessie's van was rolling down the road and stopped a short distance from the arena. Daisy wrenched her arm from his grasp and said, "Just leave me alone, Ryder. Please," and hurried toward the house. She was grateful he'd be too busy to come after her. She was thankful she could head for her room and be alone to have a good cry.

The town of Whitehorn was settling down for the evening as Audra Westwood freshened her lipstick. A plastic surgeon had added some lushness to her lips, and she liked the look, though now and then she thought about having her hair dyed back to its natural reddish-brown color. Running her finger down her nose, she was glad she'd had that bump removed, too, even if it had been her adoptive mother's idea. That woman never thought she did anything right, or ever looked quite good enough, or ever could *be* quite good enough. And if Felicia Westwood could see the dump she was living in now…

Micky Culver had convinced Audra to move back in with him. No, "blackmailed" her into it would be a better word. He knew what she'd done—he'd seen her hit Christina Montgomery with that rock. When he'd confronted her with all of it, she'd informed she didn't want to get him involved in the trouble.

But he'd told her in a warning voice there'd be no trouble if they were back together again.

His trailer was a dump, and she couldn't wait to leave. But she had to play nice; she had to make him believe that she still loved him.

The thing was—she didn't know how much she trusted him. Only if someone else were convicted of Christina's murder would she feel safe. Once that happened, she could leave and go anywhere she wanted. Her last visit with her "real" mother had been interesting. Lexine wanted her to find those damned sapphires and wasn't beneath using black-mail, either. Unfortunately, Audra had confessed to Lexine what she'd done to Christina Montgomery.

Still, Lexine was a "you scratch my back, and I'll scratch your back" kind of person. Audra understood that. Lexine had made a suggestion worth thinking about to help Audra throw suspicion for Christina's murder on to someone else. There was a new girl in town. People were always suspicious of and gossiped about the new people. Lexine had told her this woman's name was Emma Stover, and she was wait-ressing at the Hip Hop.

A waitress who was new in town could have a motive that no one knew about. So what if Audra called the sheriff's office and left an anonymous tip? If she put them on Emma Stover's trail, gave them the idea that someone had seen Emma up on the mountain that night...

Micky Culver stood in the bedroom doorway, watching Audra apply makeup. Damned, she'd be pretty if she let her hair grow and put some weight on her bones. But sometimes she went for days with-out eating. He didn't get it, just like he didn't get her most of the time. Standing there, watching every move she made, he combed his fingers through his mustache and goatee. He couldn't believe Audra had taken a rock to that Montgomery woman. He hated violence, and Audra knew it. She had a wild, dark side that he glimpsed sometimes, and he had to admit it fascinated him.

A kitten rubbed against his ankle, and he scooped it up, wishing they could live somewhere other than this trailer. Someday he'd get better pay than he was making in the body shop. Someday he'd give Audra a real life.

If she stayed with him.

Audra was still unaware of him as she finished with the eye shadow and, as if she'd made up her mind about something, moved with determination to the phone on the nightstand. But when she sat on the bed and lifted the receiver, she spotted him standing there.

"You're home early," she said.

"Not so early. I thought we could eat supper together."

She put the phone down.

"Go ahead and make your call. I'll wait."

With a little shrug, she responded, "I can make it later."

"We can go to that new fast-food restaurant and get some fries and a burger."

She wrinkled her nose. "I'm really not hungry."

After stroking the kitten around the neck, he put it down on the floor. It scampered to the front of the trailer, but he moved into the bedroom. "You've gotta eat, Audra. I don't want you disappearing into nothing," he said, joking, trying to make her smile.

But a look came into her eyes, a look that he knew,

as she crooked her finger at him. "I know something we can do that's a lot better than going for fast food."

The way her gaze passed over him, from his long hair, down his short-sleeved T-shirt, and the tattoos on his arms to his biker's boots, he felt a ripple of excitement race through him. He couldn't resist her when she came on to him, but he tried for her own good.

Crossing to her, he stood in front of her. "We really should get something to eat."

But as if he hadn't said a word, she gave him a sultry smile and ran her hand up his jeans-clad thigh to his crotch. "I think we should spend some quality time together, then worry about burgers and fries." Her hand smoothed over his fly, and he was aroused and hard in an instant.

With a groan, he pushed her back onto the bed, then came down on top of her. This woman was his world, and if she stayed with him, he'd do anything for her. Even hide the fact that she was a murderess.

Everyone at the dinner table at the Kincaid ranch couldn't help but notice that Daisy was miffed at Ryder. After all, she avoided looking at him, she avoided talking to him, she avoided passing him the salt. Leanne was giving him accusing looks, Cade speculative ones. Garrett just smoothed the conversation around all the tense vibrations. But afterward, Ryder knew he had fence-mending to do if he ever wanted Daisy to have a civil conversation with him again. The trouble was, first Garrett waylaid him after supper and asked how the boys from Laughing Horse were getting on, and then Rand called, asking him to cover the calving barn for a while. Two of the hands had come down with some kind of flu. So by the time Ryder got back to the house to talk to Daisy, he couldn't find her.

After he changed upstairs, he knocked on her bedroom door. When she didn't answer, he opened it and saw the room was empty.

Garrett was sitting in the living room, watching the news channel on the TV. Before Ryder could ask, the older man pointed down the hall. "In the parlor."

Ryder found Daisy in the parlor, all right, and at first he couldn't tell what she was doing. He heard music and she held a tape recorder on her stomach.

Only a dim light shone under the Tiffany shade on a tall marble-topped table. When Daisy looked up at him, he thought he saw something wonderful there for a moment. But then it was gone and her expression sobered.

Coming farther into the room, he asked, "What are you doing?"

"If I tell you, you'll think I'm crazy."

"I doubt that."

She switched off the tape recorder and set it on the table beside her. "There have been studies that show that babies react to music. So I play some most nights."

Ryder couldn't keep from smiling.

"See. I knew you'd think I was crazy."

Coming closer to her, he said gently, "I don't think you're crazy at all. I think it's a great idea. What are you playing?"

"Tonight, Mozart."

"So this baby's going to know high-brow music when he hears it?"

Her voice took on a defensive tone. "I hope to give this child a well-rounded education."

Uh-oh. If he didn't watch himself, he'd be in deeper water than he was already in. "Do you feel him—or her—kicking?"

A softness came into her eyes that he'd like to wrap up and keep. "I don't know about kicking," she said. "But I've felt movement the past few weeks."

"Could *I* feel it?"

"Maybe. Sometimes there's a little thump near the surface."

He crouched down beside her. "Can I?" He held his hand above her tummy.

She looked uncertain for a few moments, but then she nodded.

Laying his hand there, he waited.

But then Daisy took it and moved it over to the side a little. He felt the vaguest of movements. Her gaze met his, and a longing seared through him that he'd never felt before. He knew it didn't just have to do with this baby, but with this woman.

Pulling his hand back, he stayed crouched beside her. "Daisy, I'm sorry I tried to find things out about you behind your back."

"Are you? Or are you just sorry you got caught doing it?"

Grimacing, he decided one thing he liked about Daisy was that he couldn't buffalo her. "Both. I didn't do it to upset you. I want you to understand something. Cade and I came from a home where we had the best parents any kids could have. They cared for us and guided us and disciplined us and gave us room to grow. And if I ever have a child, I want to be that kind of parent."

She looked away from him, and he'd give his best saddle to know what she was thinking. But he'd never know what she was thinking if he didn't back off. He'd never know if he was the father or not unless he gave her some room. He'd discovered something important about Daisy. He couldn't coax her with charm and he couldn't push her. If he did, she'd hide from him and she might even run from him.

So he clasped her arm. "I'll let the subject of this baby's father drop for now."

That brought her eyes to his again.

"Instead of me trying to find answers, maybe you and I can work on being friends."

"Friends?"

"Yeah, you know, buddies."

She shook her head. "You and I? Buddies? Now, there's a picture."

"Everyone could use another buddy, don't you think?"

A smile broke out on her face. "I think it's hard to stay angry with you."

"Now, that's what I like to hear. Besides, a bad temper will just put lines on that pretty face of yours."

"Ryder..."

"Can't friends give other friends compliments?"

There was a rap on the doorjamb, and Ryder looked over his shoulder. Cade was standing there. "Am I interrupting?" his brother asked.

Hell, yes, you're interrupting, Ryder thought. But he couldn't say it and he didn't even know why he felt it. He stood. "Is something wrong?"

"No. Leanne and I were just talking."

"Mmm, I'll bet," Ryder said, smiling.

Cade ignored the innuendo. "We thought it would be a great idea if you gave a training clinic for the ranch this summer. We'll be getting the breeding program off the ground, and it would be a good opening to get the folks around here interested. We could advertise all the way to—"

"Whoa. You know that summertime is the busiest time for rodeos. I'm booked solid."

"We could make it worth your while," Cade coaxed.

"I'm sure you could. But it's not just the money."

"All I'm saying is that you should think about it. I know you thrive on the competition and the traveling, but it would be a break from that, a chance to do something different."

Before he could form a reply, Daisy pushed herself up from the rocker and picked up the tape recorder. "I'll let you two talk. It's time I turn in, anyway."

There was something in her voice that bothered Ryder, something there now that hadn't been there a few minutes before when they'd gotten friendly again. He didn't really have anything else specific to say to her, and he sure couldn't pull her into his arms with Cade standing there watching, so when she went to the doorway and said a quiet good-night to both of them, he let her go.

"Did you patch things up?" Cade asked him.

"Sort of."

"A clinic could be the start of something new for you, something to consider when you want to quit calf roping."

Quit calf roping? He'd never planned to do it this soon. He couldn't even imagine his life without traveling from rodeo to rodeo, without competing. But then again, he remembered the life he'd felt move under his hand just moments ago.

"Let me think about it," he told Cade. He'd never thought much about the future before, but now he might not have any other choice.

If he was going to be a father.

For a moment last night Daisy had listened to Ryder talk about his parents, about being a parent, and had her first doubts about raising this baby alone. But then Cade had come in and asked Ryder to do something normal, something different, something real. And Ryder had refused.

The thought of settling down would seem like a trap to him, she guessed. No man wanted to be trapped, even if he thought there might be some moments in that entrapment that he could enjoy. To pursue an affair, her father must have felt trapped. Or even worse, he'd found love instead of duty in someone else's arms. No matter what she felt for Ryder, she wouldn't saddle him with a burden that would make him resent her in the long run. And she simply couldn't imagine subjecting a child to on-again, off-again love from a father who was often absent.

Still, when she received a call from Cora Tallbird that afternoon, the person she wanted to tell about it was Ryder. Drawn to him in spite of her resolve not to be, she found herself walking to the indoor arena where she knew he was working with the boys from Laughing Horse. When she stepped inside, she saw two of the boys mounted on Leanne's mare, Delilah, and Ryder's mount, Lady Luck. The boys were walking the horses around the ring slowly as Ryder stood close by, supervising. Then suddenly from the middle of the ring, the other two boys were arguing. Daisy couldn't hear exactly what they were saying, but their stances and voices were angry. Immediately, Ryder walked over to them and capped each boy's shoulder. Then he crouched down between them and seemed to listen. She saw him shake his head.

Moving closer, she heard him say, "Gary will take a turn on Delilah this time and Rob on Lady Luck. The next time you come out here, if you get your chores finished, we'll switch. Understand?"

Both boys nodded.

When Ryder saw Daisy, he gave her one of those smiles that made her knees weak. He told the two boys, "Go over to the barn and tell Leanne to give you the grooming brushes. I'll be over with the horses in a few minutes."

After they hurried off, Daisy said to him, "Looks as if you have your hands full."

"I need eyes in back of my head," he joked.

"You do a good job with them." And he did. He was patient and guided them like a good teacher would, like a good parent would.

"Thanks," he said as if he meant it. "What brings you out here?"

"Cora called me. The Tribal Council approved me. I'm starting at the school on Monday. For now, it will be three mornings a week."

"And you can't wait to get started," he said knowingly.

"That about sums it up. Cora invited me to come to the school tonight—they're having a creative arts open house. All the classes are displaying their work. She thought I might like to come and get acquainted with the school and some of the teachers."

"I could drive you. Gary mentioned a couple of his drawings will be on display. He asked if I would come by tonight. It makes more sense for us to go together than separately, don't you think?"

Of course it made more sense, but she wasn't sure it was the best thing to do. It also surprised her that Ryder would give up a Friday night out to go to the school with her.

"Snow might be moving in tonight. It could start before we get back."

Was he being protective? She was torn between liking the idea and feeling uncomfortable with it. "I know how to drive in the snow, Ryder."

"Unfortunately, I don't think there's anything you don't know how to do," he said ruefully. "But what about our decision last night to try to become friends? Friends spend some time together."

Yes, friends did, and she supposed spending a little time with Ryder wouldn't hurt. After all, it was a school function. There'd be plenty of chaperons. "All right. What time do you want to leave?"

"Around six-thirty."

Daisy nodded her agreement. "Will you be coming in for supper, or will you be checking the heifers?"

"I'm off tonight, so tell Leanne to set me a place."

Daisy felt as if she could just stand there all afternoon looking into his eyes, watching the expressions on his face, talking to him. But she'd have the chance to do all those things tonight. "See you later," she said with a slight wave of her hand.

He tipped his Stetson to her. "See you later."

On the drive to Laughing Horse that evening, Ryder couldn't figure out why he felt nervous. Maybe it was because this seemed like a date—a first date.

Maybe because, in a way, he and Daisy were starting over.

He'd never given much thought to starting a relationship before. They'd always just happened. This one sort of had, too. But with Daisy he knew he had to ease into anything between them.

The sounds of kids and their parents echoed in the halls as Ryder and Daisy made their way to the cafeteria where the displays were set up. Each grade had a space. There were Peg-Board displays, pictures hanging from clothespins on lines of string, projects on tables that parents could pick up and read.

Ryder helped Daisy with her coat. His hands brushed her shoulders and she stared up at him. "Thank you," she murmured.

He was so tempted to bend his head and kiss her, but she'd be mortified if he did that here, and he knew better.

Cora came up to them while they were looking at the first grade's display. "I'm so glad you could come. I have several teachers who want to meet you and talk with you. I'm afraid everyone wants to take advantage of your expertise."

Ryder saw Daisy's eyes light up, and he realized her work made her feel valuable.

At the second graders' display, Daisy tilted her head to study the pictures hanging on a string. "I think children's artwork is so expressive. It tells you exactly what they're thinking."

To Ryder, the pictures looked like primitive line drawings with colors splashed here and there. But from the way Daisy was studying them, he knew they were more. Her background was so different from his. He'd never even entertained the idea of going to col-

lege, and he couldn't imagine being cooped up in a
classroom any more than he'd had to be. High school
graduation had been a highpoint in his life because it
meant he was finished with formal education. He'd
always been an outside, let-me-get-my-hands-on-it
kind of kid, and school had been stifling with its rules
and regulations and assignments that seemed to make
no sense. But all of it apparently made a lot of sense
to Daisy.

When a woman approached her, introduced herself
as the fourth grade teacher and the two of them started
talking about methods of teaching reading, Ryder felt
estranged from the subject and the conversation. He
pretended to be studying the projects on the display
table, but listening to the women's discussion, their
talk of theories and strategies, left him wondering
how high Daisy's IQ was. This was another side of
her he'd never seen. She was confident in her knowledge, in her ability to grasp any concept, in herself.
He suddenly thought about the conversations he'd had
with her, spanning the wedding and the time he'd
been here. They seemed so mundane, basic, ordinary.
Maybe he'd bored her. Maybe his lack of an education was another reason she didn't want to tell him
he was the father.

Still listening, he picked up a booklet one of the
children had made. Each page had a picture of a different animal, drawn in markers and crayon.

He heard the fourth grade teacher say to Daisy,
"We have to give the children something to aspire
to. They think this reservation is all there is to life,
especially the ones whose fathers can't find work and
have decided that drinking is the answer to life's
problems."

"We have to awaken their inherent curiosity," Daisy agreed. "If they're curious about the bigger picture, they'll want to explore it, or maybe want to become part of it."

The other teacher nodded. "I want to see them become engineers and physicians and teachers and physicists, rather than aspiring to owning a horse someday and learning to rope calves."

Ryder went perfectly still and waited for Daisy's comment.

It came quickly. "We have to teach them that education never stops, that whether they get a job flipping burgers or working as a cowhand, they can still be reading and learning and preparing themselves for something better."

Something better, Ryder thought. What if being a cowhand was all a man wanted? What if the competition and winning a prize and living in the moment were all that mattered?

When Cora brought another teacher over to introduce her to Daisy, Ryder moved away. Maybe this problem with Daisy wasn't so easy to solve. Maybe being friends with her wouldn't get him any further than being lovers had.

Suddenly he felt a tug on his elbow. Gary Eagle stood beside him with a grin on his face. "You came."

"I said I would," Ryder said seriously.

Gary motioned to a display on the other side of the room. "C'mon. Let me show you what I did."

Ryder followed the boy, glad for his enthusiasm, knowing instinctively that Gary's energy could be channeled in a positive direction, much easier than the other three boys.

Punch and cookies and coffee were set up at the front of the room. But after Ryder looked at Gary's drawings and told him what a good job he'd done, he suddenly felt the need to leave.

Daisy and all the other teachers belonged here. The parents and kids belonged here. He didn't.

Daisy had been right that the two of them were very different. He hadn't realized just how different until tonight. Maybe tonight he'd finally seen how he looked to her. He was good with a rope and a horse, and that was about it. Where she valued education, he'd dismissed it in favor of living life. She knew exactly what children needed—a stable home, moral values, a place to belong. He was a nomad, with no place of his own. Staying on Rimrock Ranch had been easy, a stopping place when he needed one. He'd never taken responsibility for having his own place, keeping it, financing it. And as far as women went…

Sure he respected them. Sure he'd made certain they'd had as much fun as he had. But what did it say about him that he'd known so many he couldn't remember all of their names? If he was the father of Daisy's child—and he was fairly certain he was—he finally realized why she wouldn't admit it.

She didn't think he was fit to be a father…and maybe she was right.

Nine

On Monday evening after supper, Daisy helped Leanne put away leftovers, certain something was wrong with Ryder. He'd been quiet and distant ever since they'd attended the creative arts open house at the school. When she'd finished talking to teachers and looking at displays Friday night, she hadn't been able to find him. Checking where their coats had hung, she'd noticed his was gone. Putting hers on, she'd gone outside and found him staring up at the sky. He hadn't given any explanations, just asked if she was ready to leave. On the drive back to the ranch, he'd switched on the radio, and they'd hardly talked. He hadn't sought her out or given her a smile or joked with her once over the weekend, and she didn't know what was wrong.

"Ryder's been awfully quiet the last couple of days," Leanne said as she wrapped biscuits in tinfoil.

"I know."

"Do you know what's wrong?"

"He hasn't given me the chance to ask him."

Leanne studied Daisy speculatively. "So you care if something's wrong?"

Tread carefully, she warned herself. "I care if something's wrong, just as if I'd care if something were bothering you or Cade or Garrett."

"Mmm."

If the sound was supposed to mean something, Leanne didn't tell her what.

"Plans are in the works for Ryder to drive to the Bar W up near Mosby on Saturday to choose some colts for Cade," Leanne informed her. "I'll bet he'd like some company."

"He hasn't said anything," Daisy responded.

"Maybe he thinks you wouldn't be interested."

"I'm not just going to invite myself along."

Leanne put the biscuits in the bread box. "Why not?"

"I'm not like you, Leanne. I can't—"

"Assert yourself? That's hogwash. I've seen you do it plenty of times, though it's usually for somebody else." After a few moments Leanne asked her, "Do you want to go with him?"

She'd missed him the last few days. She'd missed him just being around her. "A change of scenery would be good," Daisy answered noncommittally.

Leanne blew out a loud breath. "Right. You have no interest in the man whatsoever, just the scenery. Saying I buy that, which I don't, what's the problem with just asking Ryder to take you along?"

Maybe she was afraid to find out what was troubling him. Maybe she was afraid that it had something to do with her. Still, she'd like to spend some time with him, even if they just drove and didn't talk. There was something about Ryder that made her feel...satisfied when she was with him, never mind excited, a bit breathless, and altogether uncertain of everything she had decided—much of the time.

Not wanting to seem too eager, she opened the dishwasher and began loading the dishes inside. "I'll think about it."

But she'd already made a decision.

Three hours later she heard Ryder come up to his room. Going to her door, she opened it just as he opened his. "Hi," she said, testing the waters.

"Another session with Jimmy tonight?" he asked.

She nodded and then decided to jump in. "Leanne tells me you're going to drive to Mosby on Saturday."

"That's right."

"Would you mind some company? I mean, if you really want to go alone, I don't have to go."

After a pause he responded, "It'll be a long trip—two hours up, checking out his stock, another two hours back. And we can't leave until around two. The owner of the place, Mr. Wharton, won't be there until four."

"That's all right. As long as we can stop if I have to stretch."

"According to Cade, there's not much between here and there. Just a couple of two-bit motels and diners. But we could always stop for a drink at one of them."

He certainly didn't seem enthusiastic about taking her along. She didn't know what had happened between them, but something had. "Never mind, Ryder. I don't have to go." She turned toward the refuge of her room.

But he caught her elbow. "Daisy, it's fine if you want to go. Really. Having someone along will make the drive seem shorter."

The dark intensity of his eyes told her of turmoil there. Maybe riding along with him on Saturday would help her understand it. "All right. I'll plan on leaving around two, then."

Releasing her elbow, he nodded, then mumbled, "I'm going to turn in. I'll see you in the morning."

Something was definitely troubling him, and she was determined to find out what it was.

Stretched out on the sofa in the second-floor sitting room of the bunkhouse, Gil Watts watched an old movie with the sound on the TV turned down low. All of the other hands had turned in, except for Jimmy Mason. Gil had seen the boy leave around ten and wondered where he was going. He'd followed him and spotted Daisy Harding letting Jimmy in the back door of the big house. It didn't make sense—unless Jimmy was doing some kind of chores for her. There couldn't be anything else going on. Not with Redstone at Daisy's shoulder every time he turned around.

Redstone. That Indian got his goat.

Hearing footsteps on the stairs, Gil sat up, thinking about meeting Jimmy in the hall, just to shake him up. Maybe he'd spill what he was doing up at the Kincaid place. Then he heard the footsteps go back downstairs again. Curious, he walked down the hall to Jimmy's room. Listening at the top of the stairs, he heard the rattle of plates and the clank of silverware. Maybe Jimmy had decided to get himself something to eat.

Gil saw the door to Jimmy's room standing open, and he took a step inside. On the bed sat a couple of books and a box of cards. Really intrigued now, Gil went over to the bed to take a look. Opening one of the books, he saw simple words: "a big red ball." On the next page "a blue ball." When he opened the box of cards and saw pictures with words underneath and particular letters underlined, something clicked.

More than once Gil had heard Jimmy ask someone when it was his shift to check the heifers. The schedule was always posted on the back of the barn door. Then before Christmas, there'd been that memo with their checks about when they'd receive the first pay of the new year. Jimmy had said he'd lost his and asked him what it had said.

Jimmy Mason couldn't read! It looked as if Daisy Harding was giving him lessons on something he should have learned years ago.

So Ryder Redstone's sidekick couldn't even read a book on the subject of training horses. Did Redstone know? He must if the kid was in and out of the big house. Still, he'd bet Jimmy wasn't too eager to have many people find out about it.

What if he thought his hero had spilled the beans?

Gil Watts had a father who'd told him over and over again how lazy Indians were, how they belonged on the reservation, how they shouldn't keep company with white folks. Gil had listened to his father, but his sister hadn't. At eighteen, she'd married one. Three months later, he'd left her high, dry and pregnant. Gil had no respect or tolerance for Indians, whether they were descendants of the Kincaids, like Cade Redstone, or not.

If he could make Ryder Redstone's life here uncomfortable, maybe Ryder would go back to where he came from, and Gil could take over the horses again. They'd demoted him in favor of a redskin who didn't even belong, and he was tired of sitting back and taking it.

All Gil had to do was let it slip to a hand that he'd

heard a rumor that Jimmy couldn't read. As fast as gossip traveled, everyone would know it, and Jimmy would think someone he trusted had let the cat out of the bag—either Ryder or Daisy.

Either way, Ryder would be uncomfortable.

Either way, Gil would get a little of his own back.

He left Jimmy's room, leaving everything the way he'd found it.

When Ryder stepped into the bunkhouse the following day for lunch, the raucous sounds of men's laughter filled the large kitchen. Jimmy Mason seemed to be in the thick of it. Cookie, the cook, slapped the boy on the back. "No wonder you got me sugar instead of flour when I sent you for supplies."

Another hand cracked, "Kind of old for readin' lessons, aren't you?"

A third hand gibed, "No wonder you don't drive anywhere but on the ranch. You don't have to worry about street signs or road signs here."

Jimmy's face was crimson, and he looked as if he didn't know where to turn. Then he saw Ryder standing in the doorway, and his embarrassment changed to anger.

Turning away from the hands and their comments and laughter, he grabbed his jacket, brushed past Ryder and hurried out the door.

Gil Watts commented, "Looks like he's not staying for lunch."

Ryder spun on his heels and went after Jimmy. The boy had taken off as if the devil were after him, and he was almost at the barn when Ryder caught up to him. "Jimmy, wait. They don't mean anything by it. They just don't have anything better to do."

Jimmy's face was mottled with red now, and his hands were balled into fists at his sides. "You promised you wouldn't tell."

"I didn't!"

"Only Miss Daisy and you knew. She wouldn't tell anyone. It was you."

"Jimmy, I swear I told no one. I wouldn't do that to you."

But Jimmy wasn't listening. "Don't pretend you're my friend, because you're not. You're like all the rest." Then he took off into the barn and slammed the door.

Ryder wanted to go after the boy to convince him somehow that he wasn't the one who let the secret out. But Jimmy wasn't in the mood to listen, and Ryder didn't know what else to say.

Not having the stomach for lunch anymore, he headed toward the calving barn. When had life gotten so damned complicated?

Glancing over at Ryder on Saturday afternoon, Daisy tried to make conversation again. They'd been traveling for about an hour, but Ryder hadn't responded to her forays into small talk.

Trying once more, she said, "I guess Cade told you that he and Leanne are going to Billings the weekend after next for the horse auction and are staying overnight?"

"He told me."

"Leanne's excited about it. She and Cade really haven't been alone that much lately."

Ryder didn't respond to that.

"She wants to throw Cade a birthday party next Sunday and asked me to help. It'll be a surprise party. Did she talk to you about getting him away from the ranch for a couple of hours?"

"Not yet."

With a sigh Daisy thought, If the easy stuff won't get him talking, maybe something she was worried about would. "Jimmy didn't show up for his lesson again last night."

Ryder gave her a quick sideways glance.

"He's been pretty upset," she continued. "He said you told everyone he couldn't read."

The set of Ryder's jaw and the tense line of his mouth should have warned her not to press. But she didn't want Jimmy to give up. "Did you?"

Ryder's hands stayed tight around the steering wheel. "I didn't tell anyone."

"Did you tell Jimmy that?"

"He wouldn't believe me. He was too angry."

"I don't think he's as angry as he is hurt. He likes you, Ryder, and looks up to you."

"I never asked to be somebody's role model."

There was a bitterness in Ryder's voice that was unlike him, and she decided not to pursue the subject. Whatever was bothering Ryder seemed to be eating at him, but she could tell that nothing she said would change his mood right now.

On the way to the Bar W, they stopped once at a convenience store where Daisy used the bathroom and stretched her legs while Ryder bought himself a soda and her an apple juice. When he handed it to her, she smiled at him. "Thanks. You know my taste."

"In juice," he muttered, puzzling her further.

She caught his arm when he would have swung around to go back to the truck. "Ryder, what's wrong?"

"Nothing's wrong, Daisy." He pulled his arm from her grasp. "I heard a weather report this morning. It's supposed to start snowing later. I just want to get this job done and get back."

She doubted if the idea of snow would put him in this kind of mood. After all, he'd been in it for over a week.

They climbed back into the truck and started driving again. This time she switched on the radio. Maybe it would release some of the tension zipping between them in the cab.

The Bar W welcomed them with a wooden arch that stretched across the road. It looked to be a larger operation than even the Kincaid ranch, but the focus was horses, rather than cattle. Both Mr. and Mrs. Wharton greeted them, and when the couple saw she was pregnant, Mrs. Wharton offered, "Come on into the house with me while the men go into the barn. We'll have tea and stay warm."

"I don't want to put you to any trouble," Daisy said.

"No trouble at all. You can keep me company. Women folk aren't so easy to find."

An hour passed easily as Daisy talked to Mrs. Wharton, listening to the history of the ranch and how they'd gotten started breeding Appaloosas. They were sipping second cups of tea when snow began falling. After Daisy used the bathroom, Mrs. Wharton showed her through the rest of the house. It, too, was even larger than the Kincaid house, and there were pictures everywhere of the family, which Mrs. Wharton explained in detail.

The idea of generation after generation growing up in the same house appealed to Daisy. There was a permanence to those kinds of roots. She looked with interest at the portraits of past Whartons to present-day ones, liking the idea of history hanging on the walls. Another hour passed as they walked from room to room.

Finally Ryder and Mr. Wharton came back inside. Ryder's expression was troubled.

"You're welcome to stay for supper," Mrs. Wharton said.

"We'd like that," Ryder answered. "But there's already four inches of snow out there, and we have a long trip back. We'd better get started."

"Four inches?" Daisy hadn't looked outside recently.

"It's coming down hard and fast, so I think we'd better leave now."

Mrs. Wharton brought Daisy her coat, and Mr. Wharton took it from his wife, helping Daisy into it. "I hope your brother likes what you chose," the older man said to Ryder.

"I'm sure he will. You've got a fine operation here, Mr. Wharton. I'll tell Cade he should come up and look around himself."

"You do that. He's welcome anytime."

After a round of goodbyes, Ryder led Daisy out to the truck and opened the door for her.

"They're nice people," she remarked.

He didn't comment, just waited for her to get inside. Apparently his mood hadn't changed during the time he'd spent with Mr. Wharton.

Darkness had already set in as they drove away from the Wharton place, with the windshield wipers trying to keep up with the amount of snow falling. The truck handled well, but Ryder's expression was serious, and she had no clue as to what he was thinking. As they turned onto the main highway, the truck's wheels spun, and Ryder swore. Daisy protectively folded her hands over her stomach.

Snow covered the truck, swirling in front of the headlights. After another hour, at least six inches covered the road, and Ryder was driving slower and slower. They were surrounded in a world of white and could hardly see through it. Daisy kept glancing at Ryder, wanting to reassure him somehow, but knowing there was nothing she could say that would make the weather better or the trip easier.

"When will Cade get his new horses?" she asked, hoping to dispel some of the tension.

"Wharton said he'll have his men deliver them this week sometime."

"Are you pleased with what you found?"

"Cade will be."

Taillights came into view in front of them, and Daisy breathed a small sigh of relief. At least they knew someone else was out in this, too. They followed the truck for a few miles, but as they rounded a curve, it fishtailed and swerved sideways. Only Ryder's expertise kept them from plowing into the truck as they came to a shuddering stop. The truck straightened itself, then headed south again.

Ryder's vehicle was sitting in the middle of the road. Pulling back into their lane, he started forward again, but he looked over at her. "Are you all right?"

"I'm fine."

She didn't know how much longer they traveled. It seemed like hours. But she knew it wasn't when Ryder put on his turn signal. She could make out faint lights up ahead.

"Are we stopping?" She was surprised, because the way the snow was falling, it could collect another couple of inches if they went inside for something to eat.

"We're stopping, all right. For the night. This is a motel."

"A motel?"

"If I were traveling alone, I'd keep going, but I can't take the chance with you."

His voice was curt, and she felt like the burden she'd never wanted to be. "If you want to keep going, keep going. Just pretend I'm not here."

But he was resolute. "We're stopping. Hopefully we'll be warm and safe until the snowplows come through. There's a diner across the road. I'll get us something to eat after we check in."

Hurt by his attitude, she said, "Ryder, you don't have to take care of me."

"And just who's going to if I don't?"

Stung by his words, tears welled up in her eyes. But she wouldn't let him see them.

"Stay put," he said as he parked alongside of a snow-covered pickup. "I'll get us checked in. I just hope they have something. I'll leave the truck on and the heater running. Crack your window a little."

After he jumped out of the truck, she wiped the tears from her cheek and told herself she shouldn't care what mood he was in, she shouldn't care what he was thinking, she shouldn't care what was troubling him.

But the problem was—she did.

He was back in less than ten minutes. "We got the last room," he said as he got in and turned off the ignition. "They only have ten rooms. The heater's not working in one of them, the toilet's clogged up in another and the rest have been taken by folks stranded like we are."

"But we can't stay in the same room." She couldn't imagine spending the night with Ryder...or maybe she could.

"There are two double beds, Daisy. And I'll certainly make sure I stay in mine if that's what you're afraid of."

"I'm not afraid," she retorted indignantly. "It's just not..."

"Proper? You and I passed proper a long ways back." Then he got out of the cab, slammed his door, came around and opened hers.

When he offered her his hand, she snapped, "I can get out by myself."

He looked surprised for a moment, then just stood back as she stepped out into the mounting snow. After he was sure she was safely on her feet, he closed her door and locked the truck with the remote. Then he tried to take her arm.

She yanked away from him. "I can manage. What room are we in?"

"Seven."

Since there were only ten rooms, theirs wasn't hard to find, and she waited while he unlocked the door. Crossing the threshold, she found the light switch and flipped it on. It was your usual, cheap, roadside motel, with two double beds, a dresser, TV, and not much else. But it looked clean, even though it seemed as cold inside as outside.

Ryder went over to the heater under the window. "Let's make sure this works." Flipping it on, he held his hands over the fan until he felt warm air. "At least we'll be warm." His voice sounded relieved.

The day was catching up with Daisy, and she suddenly felt more tired than she'd felt in a long while. Nauseous, too. It was probably just the tension from the ride. Going over to one of the beds, she sat.

"I'd better go get us something to eat before that diner closes."

When tears came to her eyes again, she blamed it on hormones. "I should never have come with you today. You should have just told me you didn't want company. You should have just told me you'd rather be alone."

Ryder heard the quiver in her voice and cursed himself for some of the things he'd said, for the black mood that had plagued him since last Friday night at the school. When Daisy had asked him about coming along today, he couldn't say no to her. In spite of the turmoil inside him, he still wanted to be with her. He'd never wanted to hurt her feelings, and it looked as if he had.

The room wasn't large, and the two beds had less than two feet between them. He lowered himself onto the bed across from her, his knees almost touching hers. "You aren't a bother. I might like to think I'd keep going if I were alone, but that would be stupid. And I'd be stuck here with no one to share dinner with."

When she looked up at him, he saw the slight sheen in her eyes, and he cursed himself again. "Look,

Daisy. I know this is the last place you want to be. But it'll get warm in here eventually, and I'll get us some food. You really will be all right tonight. I'll stay way over on the bathroom side.''

Tilting her head, her gaze passed from his hair to his lips, then back to his eyes. ''I'm not afraid to be here with you, Ryder. It's just…you seem to be upset with me, and I'm not sure why. Being cooped up here together isn't going to help.''

Upset with her? Is that what she thought? ''I'm not upset with you, Daisy. I'm just trying to work out some things in my head.''

''What things?''

All of it was raw, and he was feeling too vulnerable to let his fears out in front of her and have her confirm them. ''Let's just say life in general. I think we should make a pact not to talk about anything heavy tonight. Is it a deal?''

''I suppose. Just one thing first…''

''What?''

''I believe you didn't talk to the hands about Jimmy.''

If they weren't in a motel room with beds that were all too inviting, he'd take her into his arms and kiss her. But he couldn't trust himself to let her *out* of his arms if he did. Standing, he crossed to the door. ''Thanks, I appreciate that. Now give me an idea of what you'd like to eat, and I'll go see what I can find.''

Less than a half hour later, snow-covered from his return trek across the highway, he knocked on the door. ''Daisy, it's me.'' He'd told her to lock the chain lock behind him, and she had. He heard her undo it, then open the door. His bag was overflowing with plastic containers and lidded cups.

"My goodness! How much did you buy?"

He laughed, shrugged off his coat and hung it in the closet, putting his hat up on the shelf. "I have two turkey dinners with stuffing, mashed potatoes, cranberry sauce and green beans, along with salads and four pieces of coconut cake. Coffee for me. Tea for you."

She laughed. "Four pieces of coconut cake?"

"The owner of the diner isn't expecting many more people tonight, and I don't think he wanted his cake to go to waste. We can eat it for breakfast."

Her smile was wide, and she looked much more relaxed than when they'd arrived.

"So are you ready for a feast?" he asked.

"I'm not really very hungry."

He was going to see that she ate, and that she ate well. Hoping the smell of the food would tempt her, he cleared off the nightstand between their beds, putting the light on the floor and the phone beside it, then opened the containers on the table. "Your gravy's on the side. I didn't know how much you'd want on."

"You thought of everything."

There wasn't anything mocking or sarcastic about her tone, and he responded, "I tried to." He would have invited her to sit on his bed with him, but was afraid she'd take it the wrong way. So instead, they both propped themselves up against their headboards and gazed at each other over the food.

"C'mon, you've gotta eat something." He waved to all of it.

Picking up a plastic fork, she poked a small bite of

turkey and put it into her mouth. "This is good," she said after a moment.

Relaxing a little, he took a forkful of his.

"I called Leanne so she wouldn't worry," Daisy said.

"Knowing Leanne, she probably made some kind of wisecrack about a motel room."

"Actually, she didn't say much."

Something in Daisy's voice made him ask, "What did she say?"

"She just told me to be careful."

Careful. He was afraid they were beyond careful. But he'd told her they weren't going to talk about anything heavy tonight, and they weren't. He was pleased to see she was taking another bite of meat and adding a dollop of mashed potatoes to it.

"Do you mind if I ask you a question?" he asked.

"It depends on the question." She took a tentative sip of her tea.

"You told me you didn't fit in when you were a kid, that you didn't find your place until you started teaching. Why did you feel that way?"

It seemed to be the last question she'd expected, and she looked down at the food and thought about it.

"You don't have to tell me," he said. "I just wondered."

Her gaze met his. "Rand was the firstborn. He got good grades, he was an athlete, he seemed to know what Dad wanted and when he wanted it. For as long as I can remember, he trailed after Dad around the ranch, and Dad always told him how proud he was of him. Leanne, on the other hand, was the baby. She demanded attention and got it. She went from as cute as a button to the prettiest girl in her class.''

''And you?'' Ryder prompted.

''I was just average all the way around, except when it came to my studies. I knew I couldn't compete with Rand, and didn't try. And I didn't mind when Leanne wanted attention, because that meant I didn't have to prove anything to anybody, and I could sort of sit back. But that happened more and more, and I found myself spending a lot of time alone. It was my own fault.''

''That didn't change as you got older?''

''I had friends at school, but studies took up most of my time.''

''What about boys?''

She ate a forkful of stuffing and shrugged. ''I was backward. They didn't notice me.''

''Not backward. Probably shy,'' he suggested. ''But I would think they'd see through that.''

''They weren't interested in seeing through anything. They wanted girls who were…more experienced.''

Remembering his teenage years, Ryder thought that maybe Daisy was right. But now… He was looking at things differently. Daisy had never been with another man before him, and that meant something.

After she started on her salad, Daisy asked, ''What about you and Cade? What were you like as kids?''

''Cade was pretty quiet, got better grades than I did, but we stuck together most of the time.'' Then seeing that Daisy was still eating the longer he talked, he kept at it, telling her about growing up on their parents' spread in Gilas, Texas, near San Antonio, about camping trips he and Cade and their dad had taken to Big Bend, about how he and Cade had once made a pot of chili that was so hot both of their parents cried over it, about how they worked on the ranch before and after school, sharing the load with their parents and liking the work even though they grumbled about it.

By the time he finished talking, he saw that Daisy had finished more than half of her dinner.

After they set aside the main course for the coconut cake, Daisy asked, "Can I ask you a question?"

"Turnabout is fair play," he said with a smile.

"It's kind of personal, but I just wondered—did your mother ever talk about Cade's father much?"

"She doesn't like to talk about the past. Before my dad, anyway. But she bore no ill feeling toward Larry Kincaid. That's Garrett's son, Cade's father. She'd been married to a man who was abusive, and Larry gave her sympathy and solace. He also gave her enough money to leave Montana and get a divorce. When she moved to Gilas, she found herself pregnant with Cade and eventually married my dad. She was honest with him about everything. Years later, she wrote to Larry and told him about Cade but that she didn't expect anything from him or his family."

"It sounds as if she was fortunate to have met your father."

"They both think that's true," Ryder said with a smile.

They talked longer about the history of the Kincaid ranch, the trouble it had seen, and how wonderful it was that Garrett wanted to make the ranch a touchstone for the grandsons he'd never known. They wondered if Garrett would ever locate the so-called seventh grandchild, to make his family complete.

After they fell into a relaxed conversational lull, Ryder broke it. "I guess we'd better turn in. I'd like to leave tomorrow morning as soon as we can. With the snow, there'll be extra work at the ranch."

"It won't take long to get ready for bed. We don't have anything to get ready with," she said with a smile.

"Do you want to take the bathroom first?"

She nodded.

While Daisy went into the bathroom, Ryder cleaned up the remains of their meal, setting aside the extra cake for the morning. When she came out, he motioned to the bed. "If you want to get undressed and slip under the covers, I won't turn the light on when I come back in."

Her cheeks reddened a bit, and she didn't say whether she would or wouldn't.

In the bathroom Ryder decided to wait until morning to shower, and stripped down to his briefs. When he crawled into the bed, he couldn't help but wonder if Daisy had undressed. He couldn't help but wonder what she'd look like naked now that she was pregnant.

They lay there in the dark and the silence, and he remembered Leanne's warning to her. *Be careful.*

"Daisy?"

"Mmm-hmm?"

"I want you to know something. I never have unprotected sex. Never. So if you're worried about the night we were together, you don't have to be. With you...that was the first time I wasn't prepared."

After a short silence when his heart seemed to be beating much too fast, Daisy responded, "Thanks for telling me."

Silence settled between them again, and Ryder wished he was holding her in his arms, wished that they could sleep together if nothing else. But it wasn't a good idea. "Good night, Daisy."

"Good night, Ryder."

He fell asleep, remembering the sound of his name on her lips.

Ten

Awakening in the middle of the night, Ryder stared up at the ceiling, aware of Daisy in the bed less than six feet away. As morning light appeared in the crack between the curtains, he wondered if he was crazy for what he was thinking, or whether it was truly a possibility. There was only one way to find out whether she thought he was fit to be a father or not: he'd ask her to marry him.

The concept of marriage was as foreign as the concept of settling down, but he would have to make changes if he was going to be a parent. There was no doubt about that. If he asked Daisy to marry him, he'd not only find out if he was fit to be a father, but if she said yes, he'd know he *was* the father.

"Daisy, are you awake?"

"Is it time to get up?" she mumbled.

"The snowplow went through about an hour ago. If the truck can make it to the road, we'll be fine." He sat up and looked over at her. Her shoulders were bare, and she looked sleep-tousled and so beautiful. He surely didn't want to stay on his side of the room. But he knew he had to; he knew he had to make this easy for both of them. "I'll go into the bathroom first so you can get dressed."

She was making sure the blanket covered everything but her shoulders. "All right. Thanks."

Slipping out of bed, he wondered if she watched as he strode into the bathroom and went inside. He'd like to think she'd be as curious about him without clothes as he was about her. He didn't come out of the bathroom until he'd given her long enough to dress.

She was peering between the curtains.

"Your turn," he said lightly.

With a shy smile, she ran her fingers through her hair. "I wish I had shampoo and a hairdryer, but I guess it can wait until I get back."

"You look just fine to me."

Their eyes met, and Daisy blushed. Then she went into the bathroom and shut the door.

Ryder paced while he waited, thinking about yesterday. After their conversation last night, he understood her better. She grew up thinking she wasn't special or even pretty. That was ridiculous. Her beauty was the type that would never fade because it was inside of her. He also realized that last night, he'd felt something for her he hadn't felt for a woman before—friendship. The desire was still there of course, but he *liked* her.

Most of all, he wanted to be the father of her baby so badly that it hurt.

When she came out of the bathroom, he was waiting, and he motioned to the bed. "Sit down for a minute, okay?"

Giving him a puzzled look, she did as he suggested.

He found himself pacing again. "Daisy, I've been thinking a lot about something." He stopped and looked at her. "The best thing for you would be to give your child a name. Marry me."

At first her eyes widened, her mouth rounded, and

then she hopped to her feet. "Marry you? Are you out of your mind? Why would you even suggest such a thing?"

"Because you need support. You shouldn't raise a child alone."

"And marrying you would solve that, with you traveling from rodeo to rodeo?"

He hadn't put much thought into the alternative yet. "Your child would have a name."

"He or she already has a name—my name. I would never marry a man who would propose to me out of nobility or...duty. And that's what you're doing."

"Daisy, listen—"

"No, Ryder. I'm not going to listen. There's only one reason I would marry a man, and that's for love." She went to the closet for her coat. "Don't you think we'd better start back?"

Ryder understood an unequivocable "no" when he heard it, and he certainly wasn't the kind of man to beg. If she didn't want him, if she didn't think he was fit to be a husband or a father, fine.

But as he put on his jacket, in his heart he knew it wasn't fine. And as he picked up the bag with the coconut cake, he decided his heart had never weighed so much as it did at this moment.

On Sunday afternoon Daisy sat in the small parlor reading, thinking about finding Jimmy and convincing him to resume his lessons with her. She needed something to do, something to keep her mind off Ryder. He'd almost been his old self once they'd stopped at the motel. He'd been considerate and caring. This morning as he'd gone into the bathroom, she'd looked, admiring his body, admiring so many things about him, thinking about what he'd said before they'd fallen asleep. He'd always protected himself before. Why hadn't he with her?

And why had he asked her to marry him?

Because he thought he was the father, or because he cared for her? Maybe he loved her. If that could possibly be true...

She was reading the page in front of her for the second time when Garrett stopped in the doorway. "You seem to be no worse for the wear after getting stuck in the snow. Did Ryder take good care of you?"

"Yes, he did." But that's all she said.

Coming into the room, Garrett lowered himself into the wing chair across from her. "Tell me something, Daisy. What's keeping you two apart?"

Since she'd met Garrett, Daisy had admired his forthrightness. But today she didn't appreciate it.

At her silence, he studied her kindly. "Everyone here pretty much knows my story, and that I'm working hard to make sure the sale of this place goes through so all of my grandsons have a legacy. But do you know what one of the things that drives me is?"

She shook her head.

"Guilt."

"Why guilt?"

"Because Larry Kincaid was my son, and he apparently didn't take responsibility for the relationships he had with women. It seems as if I should have been able to do something about that."

"Children often do wrong in spite of what their parents teach them." She imagined Garrett would have been a good teacher...and a good parent.

"Maybe, or maybe things affect them that parents can't control. My wife and I had to get married. I loved her deeply, and we had fifty wonderful years together. But Larry knew the basis of our marriage, and nothing I could do would change that. You'd think love and fidelity and happiness would.''

The fact that Garrett had married his wife because of pregnancy hit a note within Daisy. ''Did you love your wife before you married her?''

''I loved Laura from the day I set eyes on her. I wanted to have money tucked away before we married, but her pregnancy just hurried the process along. Truth be told, it made me love her more. I was even more determined to build a good life for us.''

Daisy thought about that. ''That's not always the case.''

''Are you thinking about yourself?'' Garrett asked.

''Not specifically. I—'' Looking into Garrett's blue eyes, Daisy knew deep in her soul that she could trust him, that she could confide in him in a way she'd never confided in anyone. ''Neither my brother nor my sister know this, but...my parents had to get married, too.''

''I see,'' Garrett said, waiting for her to go on.

''But I don't think their marrige was like yours. When I was a teenager, my father had an affair, and it almost tore their marriage apart. My mother was afraid he never really loved her, and I can see why any woman who has to get married because of a child might wonder why the man is marrying her. How can there ever be a complete knowing that it's based on love and not duty?''

''I think that depends on the two people involved. Laura never had any doubts how much I loved her— at least, I hope she didn't. I made sure I told her every day, and I tried to show her in countless ways. She did the same for me. Just because there's an unexpected pregnancy doesn't mean the love isn't there. What happened with your parents?''

''They worked out their problems and they stayed married. My mother seemed happy afterward. But I don't know if her doubts were gone, and I don't know if they ever could be.''

Garrett leaned forward. ''Daisy, you can't make the mistake of taking someone else's history for your own. You have to make your own history and make your own life.''

Garrett's words rang with the truth of his seventy-two years. The trouble was—

She might have fallen in love with Ryder, but she didn't know if he had fallen in love with her.

Ryder's deep-seated disappointment with Daisy's answer to his proposal unsettled him. He should be glad he was off the hook. She didn't want to marry him. But still, he felt responsibility toward his child.

When he stepped into the barn, he heard voices in the tack room. Thinking he might find Cade there, he headed that way.

But when he heard his name mentioned, he stopped a few feet from the door.

''Do you know if anything happened between Ryder and Daisy again while they were gone?'' Cade asked Leanne.

''She's not talking about it any more than he is. But you know, I've been thinking about something. I think I know why she slept with him.''

''Besides the obvious reasons?'' Cade asked, amusement in his voice.

''Obvious reasons don't apply to Daisy. It was so

completely out of character for her. Then I remembered something she'd told me last summer. She was worrying about turning thirty and her biological clock ticking. She told me then she'd always wanted a baby. Maybe Ryder gave her the perfect opportunity to get what she wanted.''

''That makes sense. It explains why she won't name the father.''

Ryder felt as if someone had hit him over the head with a branding iron. Could Leanne be right? Had Daisy used him to have a baby?

Anger roiled inside of him as he thought about it. Spinning on his heels, he headed out of the barn again and tromped through the snow up to the house, fuming all the way. If that were true, he wanted to know. If that were true, then she'd planned the whole thing. If that were true, she had no intention of ever admitting who the father was.

When he crossed the entranceway, he saw Garrett coming down the hall from the parlor. ''Is Daisy down there?''

''Sure is.''

Opening his jacket, he strode down the hall, not caring what Garrett thought, not caring what he overheard. Daisy was sitting by the window, a book on her lap, but she wasn't reading. She looked up when he came in, and when she saw his expression, asked, ''Is something wrong?''

''Damned straight, something's wrong. I just overheard a conversation between your sister and my brother. They were examining the reasons why you might have slept with me.''

Her face reddened. ''Ryder, I'm sorry—''

''Oh, it gets better. Your sister suggested that you

slept with me so you could have a baby before it was too late. I want to know if there's any truth to it.''

Her cheeks became even rosier, and she looked down at the book on her lap.

"Daisy, answer me. Is it true?''

"It's true that I slept with the father of the baby to have a child. Yes.''

With a very explicit epithet, he left the room, walked down the hall and exited the back door, closing it with a loud slam.

Daisy felt so shaken that the book on her lap dropped to the floor. Ryder had looked hurt and disappointed and downright furious. If she examined it from his point of view, what she'd done was no better than a man using a woman for sex. But she couldn't blame it all on the champagne, and hoping for a child wasn't the only reason she'd slept with him. From the moment she'd met him, she supposed she'd fallen a little bit in love with him. That little bit had grown with each conversation until her attraction to him had simply taken over. She'd let it take over.

Again she remembered her mother's words that day in her bedroom. *I've always wondered if he loves me.*

The thought of marriage without love was alien to Daisy. Duty could never take its place. Neither could nobility.

It had been difficult for her to turn down Ryder's marriage proposal because she loved him so much, but she could never marry him unless he loved her.

She couldn't marry him if all that was between them was a child.

Ryder carried the bags of party supplies to the truck and shoved them into the back seat. ''Did we get everything on Leanne's list?''

It was early Saturday evening, and Daisy had come into town with Ryder as a favor to her sister. Leanne hadn't wanted to make Cade suspicious the day before his birthday party, so she convinced Daisy to go with Ryder to pick up everything she needed.

"I think so," Daisy answered Ryder, glad he finally decided to say more than one word at a time to her. The tension between them was so thick it could choke her if she let it. She hated it, but she wasn't sure what to say to Ryder to make it go away. He'd avoided her all week.

But he couldn't avoid her now, and somehow she was going to bridge this gap between them. "Why don't we go to the Hip Hop to get something to eat before we go back? You must be hungry." They'd left Whitehorn around five, after he'd finished with the horses.

"You didn't eat anything before we left?" he asked.

"No. I wasn't hungry then."

He didn't look enthusiastic about going to the Hip Hop with her. "You can't wait until we get back to the ranch?"

It was obvious he wasn't going to make this easy for her. "I can wait, but I'd like to have supper with you. I thought maybe we could talk. I want to explain…"

"I don't think there's anything to explain, Daisy."

"Please, Ryder."

He blew out a long breath. "All right."

After Ryder drove the short distance to the Hip Hop and parked, he came around the truck for Daisy.

But she'd already gotten out. They walked side-by-side into the restaurant. Though Ryder opened the door for her, he was careful they didn't touch as she passed him to go inside.

The café was crowded, but two booths emptied as they walked in. Emma Stover waved at them. "I'll have the tables cleared off in a minute. Go ahead and sit down."

Ryder slipped into one side of the booth, Daisy into the other. Emma smiled at them both as she cleared the table and then wiped it. They didn't speak as she went to get menus. They didn't speak as she took their orders. They didn't speak as she smiled and said the wait might be a little longer tonight.

Ryder just nodded.

Clearing her throat, Daisy asked, "Why did you sleep with me, Ryder?"

Taken aback for a moment, he scowled. "Because I wanted to."

"So it was an entirely selfish reason, then?"

"Look, Daisy. I didn't set out with a goal. Not like you did. And I didn't realize that I was just going to be first in a line of men until you made your dream come true."

Oh, Lord. By not telling him he was the father, she'd gotten herself into a real mess. "It wasn't like that, Ryder."

"Oh, no? Then just how was it? Because whether it was me or whether it was some other guy, you used whoever it was to get what you wanted. No wonder you were willing to give up your virginity so easily. You're just lucky you picked someone who made you enjoy the experience so you'd want to try it again."

His barbs hurt. "I didn't *plan* to sleep with you. I

never drink. I'd had three glasses of champagne. You started kissing me, and, well, I ended up in an unusual situation for me. Once I was in it, I just went with it. It wasn't premeditated. I was just so attracted to you…'' She stopped before she crossed into dangerous territory.

He looked surprised by her admission, and not quite as disgruntled. After a stretch of silence, he asked, ''So you decided to just let whatever might happen, happen?''

''Yes.''

''So what about the next time? Was it on purpose, or did that just happen, too?''

Before she could find some kind of adequate response, there was a commotion at the door. Gil Watts and two of the other hands came in, their voices unusually loud.

''Damn. They've been drinking,'' Ryder muttered.

''It's still early,'' Daisy said, her eyes on Gil.

''They probably enjoyed happy hour at the Black Boot before coming here to get something to eat.''

Watts and his friends scanned the tables and then the booths, looking for an empty spot. When Watts's gaze fell on Daisy and Ryder, he sauntered toward them. ''Aren't you two cozy?'' he remarked.

Ryder's jaw set, and Daisy could see he was trying to hold on to his temper. ''There are stools at the counter, Watts.'' Ryder inclined his head that way.

But the cowhand wouldn't be deterred from what he wanted to say. ''So you two are together *off* the ranch as well as on it.'' Some of his words were slurred. ''I heard you and Miss Daisy spent the night at a motel last weekend. Mmm-mmm.''

Now Ryder's shoulders tensed and his expression became grim. "Move on, Watts."

"Or what? Afraid I'll touch her again?" He grunted. "Neither of you is worth my trouble. You're just an Indian who knocks up white girls, and somebody needs to teach *her* better morals than laying down with a redskin."

Quicker than anything Daisy had ever seen, Ryder was out of the booth. A fist flew—she wasn't sure whose. But the next thing she knew, Ryder clipped Watts hard on the jaw. Off balance for a moment from the blow and the booze, he shouted an expletive, then went after Ryder in earnest. Soon the two of them were on the floor. Watts pinned Ryder's shoulders down, but then Ryder broke his hold and punched him in the stomach. Watts doubled over for a moment, then, enraged, struck out, punching Ryder in the ribs.

Suddenly a man wearing a black Stetson and a black jacket with an emblem on the sleeve, lunged into the middle of the two men on the floor, bracing them apart. He yelled, "Break it up. Now."

Daisy slid to the edge of the booth. "Ryder. Ryder, stop."

As soon as he heard her voice, Ryder looked at her, his expression pained.

Gil went for him again, but the officer held Gil back and Ryder got to his feet. "Do I have to cuff you two?" the lawman asked sternly, standing and waiting for Watts to get up, too.

"Cuff us?" Watts asked, scrambling to his feet. "What the hell…"

"We're going over to the sheriff's office. I'm going

to let you two cool off in jail until I settle what happened here.''

There was another round of swearing from Watts.

"Cuffs aren't necessary on my account," Ryder said tersely.

The officer looked at Daisy. "The name's Sloan Ravencrest. I'm a sheriff's deputy. Mind coming along and giving a statement?''

"No. I don't mind.'' She wasn't about to let Ryder go into that sheriff's office by himself.

"Okay, let's go.'' Sloan waited while Daisy and Ryder collected their coats, then he motioned for them to move outside.

The short ride to the sheriff's office was silent. Watts and Ryder rode in the back behind the mesh screen, Daisy up front with the deputy. At the office, Sloan let Daisy precede him up the right side of the steps separated by an iron railing, all the while keeping an eye on Watts and Ryder as they followed her inside. The wooden bench in the reception area was empty. Daisy recognized Reed Austin, another deputy, who was seated behind one of the desks.

Standing, he came forward and pushed open the low, wooden swinging gate. "Two hotheads?'' he asked.

"I'm not sure yet,'' Sloan replied. "But this one—'' he pointed to Gil "—has had too much to drink. I can smell it. Put each of them in a separate cell back there until I talk to the lady. Then I'll interview them.''

As Reed motioned to the barred door at one side of the room, Ryder said, "Wait.''

Sloan's brows arched. When Ryder reached into his coat pocket, Sloan grabbed his wrist.

"Keys," Ryder snapped. "I want to give her keys."

When Sloan backed off, Ryder took out the keys to the truck and gave them to Daisy. "Go on back to the ranch. I don't know how long this is going to take."

She accepted the keys from him, but she had no intention of using them—not until she got him out. But before she could say anything to him, Reed shepherded the two men off to the jail cells.

Sloan's expression was kind as he motioned to the bench, then sat beside her. "Do you want to tell me what happened?"

It didn't take long for Daisy to tell Sloan Ravencrest what had happened. She made it perfectly clear that none of it was Ryder's fault, that Gil had approached her before and that Ryder was protective of her.

When she was finished, Sloan's lips tipped up in a smile. "Are you sure you're not a bit biased?"

"Absolutely not."

The deputy's smile broadened.

"All right. Maybe a little. But you can ask anyone who was there and overheard. Gil provoked Ryder."

"Reed went to talk to the folks over there. We'll get the whole story one way or another."

She hadn't even noticed that Reed Austin had left. "Now what?" she asked.

"Now I'm going to talk to each of them separately. You're free to go if you want."

Shaking her head, she said, "I'm waiting for Ryder."

"And what if I decide to keep him overnight?"

"Then I'll go find a lawyer, and we'll get him out on bail."

"I can see you're one determined lady. Are you going to be okay here? This bench gets kind of hard."

"I'll be fine."

Crossing the room, Sloan unlocked the barred door and disappeared beyond. A few minutes later he came out with Ryder, pointed to the open door of the interrogation room, and they went inside.

She didn't even know if Ryder knew she was there.

Holding the keys to Ryder's truck in her hand, Daisy wondered what was going through his head. A short time later the outside door to the sheriff's office opened and Reed came back in. About the same time, Sloan emerged from the interrogation room and shut the door. "What did you find out?" he asked Austin.

"Watts goaded Redstone. It's not surprising since Watts has a chip on his shoulder where—" Reed stopped and glanced at Daisy.

Sloan said, "Just keep your eye on that door and make sure Redstone doesn't leave yet, while I talk to Watts. Then we'll wrap this up."

When Reed asked Daisy if she'd like a cup of coffee, she declined. About fifteen minutes later, Sloan returned to the reception area, then opened the door to the room where Ryder was seated. "Come on out, Redstone. Pay me two hundred dollars for disturbing the peace, and you're free to go."

Ryder stood in the doorway, his hat in his hand. "And if I don't have two hundred dollars?"

"Then I guess you'll have to spend the night with your friend Watts."

Hearing the discussion, Daisy rushed over. "I have

some money with me. Maybe together we'll have enough.''

Avoiding her gaze, Ryder set his Stetson on his head and took out his wallet. He had a hundred and fifty in assorted bills. Daisy found the additional fifty dollars he needed in her purse and handed it to the deputy.

''Well, I guess that's it,'' Sloan said. ''Unless you want to get into trouble again.''

Ryder didn't say anything but snapped his sheep-skin jacket.

Daisy went to the door and waited for him. After he opened it for her, they stepped outside. The wind blew forcefully down the street, catching the end of Daisy's scarf.

''Why did you wait?'' he asked.

''Because if they arrested you, you would have needed a lawyer and bail.''

''I thought you'd want to hightail it back to the ranch and get as far away from me as you could.''

Looking up at him, she saw his jaw was red, and she couldn't keep from touching it. ''Does this hurt?''

''Not as bad as my pride.'' Then he pulled away from her. ''Let's get you into the truck. It's too cold out here to stand and talk. Or I can get the truck and come back and pick you up.''

''Let's walk,'' she decided.

The wind buffeted them as they descended the steps, Ryder on one side of the iron railing, her on the other. Daisy hardly noticed as she thought about Ryder and what he must be feeling and thinking.

Back at the truck, she handed him his keys. He unlocked the doors, then helped her inside. After he climbed in, he switched on the ignition and the heat.

Staring straight ahead, Ryder said, "I'm sorry you were subjected to that."

She hadn't put her seat belt on yet, and she moved closer to him on the bench seat. "Gil Watts is the one who should be apologizing, Ryder, not you."

He shifted toward her. "You mean that, don't you?"

"Of course, I do. He pushed you until—"

"Daisy, honest to God, I can handle it for myself. But when he insulted you, all the anger and resentment and bitterness that's built up over the years at remarks like that just drove me out of that booth."

Her shoulder brushed his arm. "Tell me about it. About growing up."

The silence suggested he wasn't sure he should. But finally he began, "Cade and I heard remarks about us being Indians in school. He'd already been dealing with it when I came up behind him. But then it was easier, somehow, with the two of us. We stood together. We shrugged and told each other it didn't matter.

"I was in third grade when I got into a fight. It was after school, and one of the kids called my mother a name. Fights never seemed to stay between two people. Others joined in, including Cade, who was trying to help me. The bunch of us was suspended from school for three days, and at home, our parents made clear what they expected of us. They told us the next time Cade and I should walk away. We should be bigger and better than others and ignore the prejudice because we'd have to do it for a lifetime. There were no more fights after that. Cade and I respected our parents too much."

"Until tonight," she said softly.

"Yeah. Until tonight."

This time when she touched his face, he didn't pull away. "Thank you for defending my honor," she murmured.

With a low groan, he tossed his hat into the back seat and took her into his arms. His lips were hot, and he took her as if he wanted to possess her, wanted to leave his brand on her, wanted to claim her as his own. Daisy gave in to the pleasure, wondering if he'd forgiven her for her plan to get pregnant, wondering if he had any idea how much she cared about him.

When he leaned back, they were both breathing raggedly. "This isn't a good idea," he decided in a husky rasp, then put space between them and squared himself in his seat. "Do you want to stop at that new restaurant and get something to eat? It's probably best we don't go back to the Hip Hop right now."

Why had he pulled away? Because he hadn't forgiven her. Maybe he never would. "No. Let's go back to the ranch. Leanne and Cade will wonder where we are. I don't want them to worry."

"Word travels fast around here. They probably already know what happened." Turning up the defroster to clear the steamed-up windows, he directed, "Better buckle your seat belt."

Returning to her side of the seat, she fastened the belt and looked straight ahead. There still seemed to be a gulf between them, and she had no idea what to do about it.

Eleven

Ryder clapped Cade on the back as everyone in the living room called, "Surprise!" late Sunday afternoon.

Cade not only looked surprised but pleased, and his gaze went immediately to his wife who was grinning from ear to ear. Running to him, she wrapped her arms around his neck. "Happy, happy birthday!" Then she gave him a heated kiss that eventually caused whistles and hoots of laughter.

"Now *that's* a birthday present," someone called out.

Ryder couldn't help but think about kissing Daisy last night. His gaze sought and found her in the crowd of people. She was wearing the red-velvet dress again and looking so lovely…

He could have taken their last kiss a lot further, but he'd ended it because of everything that had gone before.

She'd seemed willing last night. He couldn't believe she'd stayed at the jail and waited for him, but he didn't know what to think about her, about them, about the baby. When he was around Daisy, the confusion was even worse. It was easier to keep his distance.

"Thanks, Ryder," Leanne said to him. "I don't think he suspected a thing."

"Don't talk about me as if I'm not here," Cade grumbled with a smile. Then he looked at his brother. "I can't believe you kept this a secret. You never could as a kid."

"The stakes are higher now. Your wife offered me the biggest piece of that birthday cake Daisy and I brought home last night."

"Gil's here," Leanne said in a low voice to Ryder. "I invited all of the hands."

Ryder smoothed his fingers along his bruised jaw. "That's okay, Leanne. I promise I'll behave. I got it out of my system last night. Watts is probably madder than hell because Ravencrest kept him overnight. I'll stay out of his way."

Daisy came up to Cade and gave him a hug. "Happy birthday. There are a lot of people here who want to help you add on another year."

Cade laughed. "I can see that. I guess I'd better mingle."

Leaning close to him again, Daisy murmured, "Brandon Harper's here. Leanne convinced him to come, and he's staying overnight. I don't think he's as hard and cynical as all of you say he is."

"You've met Harper?" Ryder asked Daisy, finding Larry Kincaid's third illegitimate son across the room.

"Not until today. But Cade had told me that at the reunion last summer, Brandon didn't seem to want anything to do with his new family. I think he's just being cautious."

Ryder knew Daisy listened well to anyone who talked to her. But as her gaze went back to the six-foot-tall, muscular, black-haired man standing across the room, Ryder felt jealousy at her empathy for a man who didn't need any. Brandon Harper was a millionaire, an investment banker, and from what Ryder had heard, he had the power to go along with it.

As Cade and Leanne went to talk to Brandon, Ryder found himself standing alone with Daisy. Her perfume was a breath away. That dress begged for his touch. He felt as if she'd woven some kind of spell around him, and he couldn't escape it. "Is Watts staying away from you?"

"Well away. And he's not saying much to anybody."

When Ryder looked over at the man, Watts's gaze held bitterness. "I wish I knew how to end it," Ryder said. "I wish I knew how to make him see I'm a man just like he is."

"You're nothing like he is," Daisy said vehemently.

"We're not so different, Daisy. Maybe I've just learned how to rope in my feelings better. Maybe I've just had more practice turning away from trouble instead of heading toward it."

"It's more than that. I don't feel safe around him. I do feel safe around you."

"Safe?" Ryder asked, thinking about last night's kiss, about the kisses that had gone before, about their night in bed.

Her cheeks flushed. "I know you would never hurt me."

"You're right about that," he murmured, thinking when the two of them were together, no one else seemed to exist. A party was in full swing, but it seemed far away.

"How does your jaw feel?" Daisy asked, almost reaching up to him, but then dropping her hand as if she thought better of it.

"It'll be sore a couple of days."

The electricity that pulsed between them pulled them together yet also kept them apart. Ryder stuffed his hands into the pockets of his jeans so he wouldn't touch her. He took a deep breath and raised his head so he wouldn't kiss her. When he did, he saw Gil Watts standing a few feet away, watching them.

The man didn't say a word. He just found his coat in the stack of them on the chair inside the living room door. Then he put it on, set his hat on his head and left the house.

"What happened last night is going to make it hard for Cade to keep him on, but I told him I don't want Watts fired because of me. Once I leave, everything will be fine."

Silence settled between them until Daisy said, "I convinced Jimmy to start lessons again with me tomorrow night."

"Good."

An awkwardness he'd never noticed before fell between them. "Well, I guess I'd better party. The chance might not come again anytime soon."

"And I'd better help Leanne cut the cake."

Although Ryder circulated, ate, and spoke to a lot of the guests, his mind was always on Daisy and his gaze rarely strayed from her. Far too often for his taste, he found her talking with Brandon Harper. It was easy to see Harper was a loner, though skilled at making conversation when he had to. Daisy had explained to Ryder that she'd been somewhat of a loner herself. Maybe that's why she gravitated toward Brandon, or maybe that's why Brandon gravitated toward her.

By evening the last of the guests had left. Garrett

had gone to his office to take a call, and Ryder joined Leanne and Cade in the kitchen, snitching another piece of cake and another scoop of ice cream. As he stood and dumped his paper plate in the trash bin, Leanne asked, "Could you bring those last few dishes in from the dining-room table? Then we'll have everything put away."

Going to the dining room, he stopped when he heard low voices just around the corner. There was a small sofa there by a reading lamp, and he heard Daisy's soft voice and then Brandon's deep one.

"That's all I know about it," she said with a low laugh.

"You've got a good grasp of the financial markets." Brandon's voice was admiring.

"I read a lot," she joked.

"Most women consider the subject dull or beyond their comprehension."

"I guess I'm not most women."

"No, I don't think you are."

Ryder didn't like the inflection in Brandon Harper's voice—or the coziness that was almost flirting. Wasn't it?

"Daisy, I admire what you're doing—going through with your pregnancy and raising a child on your own," Brandon said.

"I never had any doubts I wanted this child."

There was a silence, and Ryder wanted to step into the living room to observe what was happening. But he kept still.

Brandon's voice was just loud enough to carry. "My mother dumped me in a foster care system so she could be a showgirl. That doesn't give a man a balanced picture of what a woman will do when she finds herself pregnant.''

"Brandon, I'm sorry."

"I don't know why I told you that," he muttered.

"Maybe because I'm pregnant. Maybe because you've wanted to say it to somebody for a long time. Maybe because you really want to have a better picture of women than you think you have."

"Do you know what I think, Daisy Harding?" Brandon asked in a somewhat amused but serious voice.

"What?"

"You see entirely too much and too well."

Again she laughed, and Ryder wished he could make her laugh more often. He was beginning to wish so many things. Forgetting about the dishes Leanne wanted, he stepped into the living room and saw that Daisy and Brandon were sitting with only a small space between them. Her elbow was almost touching his. The jealousy that roiled inside of Ryder was so palpable, he felt as if he were turning green. But before he could get a grip on something appropriate to say, Garrett came down the hall from his office.

As Garrett approached Brandon, he smiled. "I'm so glad you're staying tonight."

"I'm still not sure I want any part of this legacy," Brandon responded.

"Why don't you come back to the office, and we'll talk about it?" Garrett looked at Daisy, then Ryder. "I'm going to be heading out myself tomorrow for a while—back to Elk Springs."

"Problems?" Ryder asked.

"No. Just tax questions. Collin needs some help

deciphering them. I'll have a chance to catch up on what's going on there, too.''

Brandon stood and lightly touched Daisy's shoulder. ''It was good talking to you. If I don't see you again tonight, I'll say goodbye in the morning.''

Ryder thought Brandon's voice carried a caressing note he didn't like at all.

Once Garrett and Brandon had gone down the hall, Ryder commented, ''Looks like you and Brandon hit it off pretty well.''

Daisy tilted her head and studied Ryder. ''He didn't seem to be talking to many people, and I just wanted to make him feel comfortable.''

''Maybe a little too comfortable,'' Ryder mumbled before he thought better of it.

Daisy stood and came over to him. ''What's that supposed to mean?''

''Nothing.''

''Just because you don't want to be around me doesn't mean other people don't.''

''I never said—''

''You didn't have to say anything. It's the way you act. And that's fine. Probably better for both of us.''

Even if Ryder thought that, he wasn't sure he believed it. ''Brandon Harper's just not your usual—''

''Ryder, Brandon and I were having a friendly conversation. I think he's smitten with Emma Stover.''

''Emma?''

''Don't look so surprised. You were flirting with her at the Valentine's Day party.''

''I was not! We were just having—'' He stopped, then went on, ''A friendly conversation.''

''Mm-hmm. And I suppose you were just having a

friendly conversation with that other woman you were holding hands with that night?''

Thinking back, he remembered Crystal clasping his hand almost in apology because she couldn't help him. Had this been bothering Daisy since then? ''If you're talking about the woman with the short, black hair, she's Sloan Ravencrest's wife. They were just married recently.''

Daisy blushed. ''Oh.''

''Daisy, I've told you before—any gossip you've heard about me is more of a tall tale than the truth.''

Leanne came into the dining room, and then peeked around the corner. ''I suppose those dishes got lost,'' she teased. Then she added, ''Cade wants to talk to you about what to look for in the horses at the auction next weekend.''

''I'll get the dishes on my way in,'' he told her.

After Ryder had gone into the kitchen, Leanne gave Daisy an appraising look. ''I guess you realize that you and Ryder are going to be here alone next weekend.''

No, Daisy hadn't realized it. But the thought of it made her feel both excited and scared. How close could she get to Ryder without getting burned?

Around seven the following Saturday morning, Leanne and Cade left for Billings. At around ten, snow began falling…and falling…and falling. By three, the winds picked up force and howled across the drifting snow, battering the house. Daisy was alone there and had thought she'd enjoy having the place to herself. But she found herself worrying about Ryder and what he and the hands were doing out in this weather. She worried about the pregnant cows and the calves about to be born.

The lights flickered a few times, and her concerns became different ones. What if the electricity went out? What if she and Ryder were stranded here in the dark?

You were stranded with him in a motel, a little voice reminded her.

The reminder didn't help. Any time she was alone with Ryder, she seemed to lose her good sense. A dark house would only add to the intimacy between them.

After searching drawers and cupboards in the kitchen, she found matches and candles. Another hour passed and the wind seemed to shriek, making the windows rattle and the house creak with strange noises. Daisy turned on the radio, but it crackled with static. She tried to read, but was too worried about Ryder and what he was doing. When the phone rang, she went to it gratefully, hoping maybe he was calling from the barn.

"Daisy, it's Leanne. Cade and I arrived safely. We didn't want you to worry. We stayed ahead of the snow and found four great horses at the auction. How's everyone there?"

"I don't know. Ryder's not back in yet."

"He will be. They're probably just making sure the animals are protected as well as they can be. They might have to lay out more feed, and there's always the calves to care for."

Just then Daisy heard noise in the foyer. "I think he's coming in."

"I'll let you go. Stay warm," Leanne said.

Daisy told her sister to do the same and then hung up.

The lights flickered again as she rushed to the entranceway. Ryder was covered in snow from his head to his feet. He moved stiffly as he shut the door, and Daisy worried about how cold he was. The snow was caked to him, icy and thick, and she could only imagine how long he'd been out in it. He wore chaps on top of his jeans, and she hoped he had long underwear on underneath.

"Are you all right?" she asked. But as she did, the small table lamp in the foyer went out and so did everything else.

Ryder swore. "I knew with the wind this might happen. I gotta go back out and get some wood."

"Oh, Ryder. Do you have to? Maybe there's enough."

He shook his head. "I checked the storage bin beside the fireplace this morning. I should have done it then, but I didn't have time. Five minutes is all it'll take." His face was red from the wind and snow, and he looked tired.

"I'll light the candles."

"Can you open up the back door for me? It's closer to the woodpile."

She nodded. As he went outside again, she wanted to throw her arms around him and hold him tight and close, and warm him with her body heat.

It was about ten minutes later when he came through the back door. She was waiting there for him with two glowing candles. "What can I do to help?"

"I don't want to track snow the whole way upstairs. In the bottom drawer of the chest, I have a pair of sweatpants and a sweatshirt. Can you bring those down for me? Oh, and a pair of dry socks."

"Sure. Do you know if there are oil lamps anywhere? They'd be better than the candles."

"After I get changed, I'll check the basement. You be careful on the stairs." Ryder took the candle she proffered and started for the living room.

"I will." His concern always touched her.

Ryder rubbed his hands together again before he laid the fire and started it. He had to get the wet clothes off. Cade had told him about the generator he could flip on if the electricity went out, but as he lit the fire, poked a log and looked at the sofa across from it, other ideas entered his mind. He knew what would happen if they had heat and lights. He and Daisy might have supper together and then go their separate ways. And suddenly tonight he didn't want to go his separate way. He wanted to get closer to her. Not even to find out the truth anymore. He just wanted to be with Daisy.

A smile slid across his lips. She probably didn't know the house had a generator, and he didn't have to make her any the wiser.

After Daisy brought his clothes downstairs, he changed in the bathroom, thinking he'd never feel warm again. He was cold down to his bones.

While Daisy lit a few more candles, he took one to the rec room in the basement. There he found an oil lamp and a camp stove. They'd be able to make some supper on that. Setting the stove up on the kitchen counter, he asked her, "How about scrambled eggs and pancakes for supper?"

"That sounds fine. But why don't you go sit by the fire and warm up? I can do it."

Even in his stocking feet he was a good eight inches taller than she was, and as he looked down at her, he felt a tenderness he couldn't begin to explain...and heat that drove the cold away. "Moving around will help me warm up."

Working together in the kitchen, they occasionally bumped elbows or hips. Ryder liked the feeling of intimacy it created. In no time at all they mixed up the pancakes and made them. While Daisy was removing the last pancake from the pan, Ryder scrambled the eggs. They cooked up quickly. Ryder took their plates to the sofa in front of the fire, while Daisy brought a mug of coffee for him and a mug of tea for herself. Ryder had never eaten dinner by firelight with a woman before, and he found himself fascinated by the way the shadows played over Daisy's face, by the closeness he felt to her, by the pleasure of being in her company with the old-fashioned oil lamp burning not far away.

"I was worried about you," she said as she finished a bite of pancake.

"Afraid I'd turn into a snowman?" he teased.

"Afraid you wouldn't realize exactly how cold it is out there, afraid something would happen..." Her voice caught.

"Hey," he said, affected by her concern for him. "Don't you know cowboys are tough?"

"You're a Texas cowboy. You have different concerns than windchill and snowblindness."

"Rand filled me in. We took shifts. Still are. But I'm not on again until first light."

Daisy was sitting about a foot from Ryder. He wanted to bridge the distance between them but wasn't quite sure how to go about it. As they ate, they talked about the differences between ranching in Texas and ranching in Montana, and Daisy told him more about growing up near Ox Bow. He described Texas sunrises, told her more about Rimrock Ranch and his parents' life there. All the while the fire crackled, and the cocoonlike feel of their small part of the living room grew stronger.

Taking her empty plate from her, he stacked it on top of his. "The temperature in the rest of the house is going to drop fast. So we'd better stay here. How about a game of cards to pass the time?"

"What do you play?"

"Anything and everything. What about you?"

"I like poker."

"Daisy Harding, where did a lady like you ever learn to play poker?"

"I have an older brother," she said dryly.

"I'll take these out to the kitchen and go get the cards. Do you want anything else? I think there are some cookies left in the jar."

She shook her head. "Not right now. But if you want some, go ahead."

"I'll wait till later. Be right back."

When Ryder returned, he not only brought a pack of cards, but toothpicks to use for betting and a down quilt to keep them warm. "I thought we might need this," he said to Daisy, settling it over her lap.

"Thank you," she murmured, looking up at him with wide, soft brown eyes.

He was so tempted to kiss her, so tempted to do more than kiss her. But they had a long night ahead of them, and he wanted her trust as well as her passion, her friendship as much as her desire. Stealing himself against urges he was used to gratifying, he sat at the other end of the sofa and then handed her the cards. "I'll let you deal first," he said with a wink.

Daisy had continued to surprise him from the moment he'd met her. Tonight wasn't any different. She was a good poker player, but as they played hand after hand, he watched subtle changes in her—the sparkle of her eyes, the tilt of her lips, the flutter of her hands—that told him when she was bluffing. By the time the fire had burned low, he'd won all her toothpicks.

"You're better than Rand," she said in a fit of pique.

"Or maybe I just know how to read you better."

Putting the toothpicks back in the box, he collected the cards, then asked, "How about a nightcap—milk and cookies?"

She smiled at him. "Sure."

They sat side-by-side, watching the fire he'd stoked, drinking, nibbling, glancing at each other now and then. Finally Ryder said, "The rest of the house is going to be pretty cold tonight. What do you want to do about sleeping?"

"I could find more covers for the beds."

"Or we could use the cushions from the sofas and make two bedrolls here in front of the fire. Even with extra covers upstairs, I'm not sure how warm we'll be."

"It *would* be warmer down here," she agreed, as if she were warring with herself.

"Good. It's settled, then. I'll get the bedrolls made up."

"You ready to turn in now?" she asked.

"I'm meeting the men at the bunkhouse around

four-thirty to decide how we're going to break up the chores. Just getting around to all the cattle with feed will take a few hours. Don't you think you'll be able to fall asleep?"

"Um, sure. I guess I will."

"I'm going to go around and check the house and make sure everything is secure. The wind could have loosened something it shouldn't. So if you want to change…"

"I think I'll just sleep in this," she said quickly. Her dark green knit shirt and slacks looked comfortable enough, but he was sure she would be more comfortable in a nightgown. Or maybe he just wanted to see her in a nightgown.

After he'd made the rounds of the house, he came back to the living room and saw that Daisy had settled on one set of cushions and had the comforter thrown over her. He'd stacked the bedrolls side-by-side, not knowing how she'd feel about that, but she hadn't moved hers away.

Before he lowered himself beside her, he said, "I know you're going to sleep in your clothes. Do you mind if I shed mine?"

"Ryder—"

"Except for the briefs."

Her eyes held to his for a few moments, and then she turned away and looked at the fire. "I don't mind."

After removing his sweatshirt, sweatpants and socks, he slid under the quilt beside her. She was well away from him on her side of the cushions, and he wished he knew how to get her into his arms. But sometimes patience paid off. He could be a patient man. Reaching to the end table, he turned down the oil lamp until it went out and the only light in the room was the glow from the fire.

Settling on his back, he folded his arms under his head and glanced over at Daisy. "Are you comfortable?" he asked her.

"Just fine."

"If you get cold, let me know, and I'll get the fire going again."

"Good night, Ryder," she said softly.

"Good night, Daisy."

It took Ryder a long time to fall asleep, aware of the woman only two feet away from him. Yet he realized it could have been a mile as he glimpsed the straightness of her back.

A few hours later Ryder felt the change in the temperature in the room and became aware of Daisy stirring. The fire had almost gone out. Rising, he said, "I'll get it started again."

Daisy had awakened because she was cold. Her feet felt frozen, and she shivered. But when Ryder opened the small door along the fireplace and she caught sight of his bare back and his powerful legs, she forgot about the cold. He'd make a beautiful artist's model, she thought as she watched the play of his muscles when he bent to the fireplace and added the logs. Everything about him was powerful and virile, and she felt the tummy-curling sensation that had nothing to do with the baby and everything to do with Ryder's physical prowess. Lying here beside him felt intimate, yet safe, too. It was so odd.

In a few minutes he returned to the bedroll and crawled under the cover. Even though the flames leaped higher, she was still chilled and shivered.

"It'll take a while to warm up in here. Why don't you come over and get warm?"

She'd been avoiding looking at him directly, but now her eyes went to his.

"I'm just talking about sharing some warmth, Daisy."

"I'm fine."

"You're stubborn, but suit yourself."

After she lay there a few more minutes and shivered again, she told herself a little warmth couldn't hurt. She didn't have to get *really* close. She inched over toward him.

"Change your mind?" His voice was deep and husky.

"My feet are ice-cold."

He chuckled. "Take your socks off. Your feet will warm up quicker."

After she did, he turned onto his side, toward her. "Okay, now put them between my legs."

"You've got to be kidding!"

"No. Go ahead. They'll be warm in no time."

Turning on her side, she lodged first one foot, then the other against him. They were facing each other, and the shadows from the fireplace flitted over his face. Her gaze fell to his lips. They were so sensual, so pleasure-giving.

"What are you thinking?" he asked.

"Nothing important."

"Your eyes got that look."

"What look?"

"The look they get when I kiss you."

Just thinking about it, being this close to him, his taut, muscled chest only inches from her fingers, made her tremble.

He reached out and slipped his hand under her hair along her neck. "I've wanted to kiss you all night."

"Oh, Ryder..." She knew her voice said she wanted it, too.

Understanding the underlying message, he urged her closer to him. A moment later his lips covered hers.

Ryder's kiss swept her along like a strong tide, inflaming her desire, letting it smolder, then inciting it all over again. It ebbed and flowed, taking, then giving, then asking for more.

Her hand was on his chest, and when she found his nipple, he groaned.

His hand left her hair, and for a moment he broke the kiss to say, "I want to touch you."

She didn't move away. She didn't say no. As his lips came back to hers, he lifted her top, feeling the skin below her breasts. In the throes of the onslaught of his tongue playing with hers, she didn't even realize he had unclasped her bra until his hand slid under her breast and then passed over it gently, caressingly, teasingly.

She felt his touch all the way to the most special place inside of her where her baby was flourishing. Their baby.

His kiss became fervently demanding as he took her nipple between his thumb and his forefinger, and she felt pleasure so keen she wanted to give it back to him. His hands slid down to her waist again, and then he broke the kiss and said, "Let me undress you."

But his words brought reality back with a vengeance. She couldn't let this happen. If she made love with him again, he'd find out how much she loved him, and she'd have to tell him this baby was his. How could she do that when she didn't know what he felt? How could she do that when their lives were so different? When he was planning to leave?

"Ryder, I can't do this. I can't." Trying to move away from him, expecting his anger or frustration, she found he wouldn't let her go.

"It's okay, Daisy. It's okay."

Gazing into his eyes, she saw that it was.

"Come here. Just put your head on my shoulder. I'll warm you up, and we'll go back to sleep."

"Are you sure?" She knew he was aroused. Her knee had brushed him and...

"I'm sure. C'mon." He held out his arm and pointed to his shoulder.

The tender expression on Ryder's face melted her, and there was no way she could refuse. Moving close to him, onto his set of pillows, he wrapped his arm around her and set his jaw on top of her head. She fell asleep that way, feeling as if she belonged there, wishing she could stay in his arms forever.

Twelve

On Sunday afternoon around supper time, Cade and Leanne came home. Rand had made sure the ranch's main access road was plowed so they wouldn't have any problems. The six inches of fresh snow had kept all the men working outside most of the day, and Daisy hadn't seen Ryder since he'd kissed her forehead and left her side early that morning.

Leanne was smiling and her eyes were sparkling as she carried her overnight case to the stairs.

"Did you have fun?" Daisy asked her.

"It was great. A horse auction and being snowed in at a motel with my husband. Who could ask for more? What about you?"

"We were fine." The electricity had come back on around 9:00 a.m. and Daisy had put away the candles and oil lamp and tidied up the living room.

"Did you and Ryder spend much time together?" Leanne asked curiously.

"Some." Daisy knew it was better to not say too much.

While Daisy and Leanne made sandwiches for a light supper, Leanne told her about the horse auction and stock she and Cade had bought. Daisy was making a salad to accompany the sandwiches when Cade and Ryder came into the kitchen.

"It seems like a long time since I saw you," Cade

said to his wife as he went over to her and gave her a kiss.

Daisy watched them, thinking about how in love they were, how that was what she wanted with Ryder. When her gaze met his, he smiled at her, and she suddenly wished they could be snowed in together again.

Cade lifted his head but kept his arm around his wife. "Rand told me that there were no lights on up here last night. Did you have a problem with the generator?"

Ryder's smile vanished and he shook his head slightly as if to warn Cade about something, but Cade went on. "I checked it before I left."

"The house is hooked up to a generator?" Daisy asked.

"Sure. I showed it to Ryder…"

Seeing Ryder's wry grimace, Daisy crossed to him. "Why didn't you tell me there was a generator?"

"I guess you wouldn't believe me if I told you I forgot."

"Not on your life."

Cade took Leanne's hand. "We're going to unpack. We'll be back in a few minutes," and he hurried his wife out of the kitchen.

"Why didn't you tell me?" Daisy asked again.

Ryder's smile was boyish, and he didn't look at all sorry about what he'd done. "I thought it would be cozier without it."

"Cozier? You're an underhanded…conniving… cowboy."

His smile slipped away. "Tell me you didn't enjoy yourself last night."

She couldn't.

"Nothing happened that you didn't want to happen, did it?" he pressed.

Again she couldn't deny it. She'd enjoyed being with him last night. She'd more than enjoyed sleeping in his arms. "That's beside the point, Ryder. You manipulated me."

"Like you manipulated me?" he asked. "When you decided to have sex with me to have a baby?"

The two didn't in any way compare and she knew it. Hers was the greater manipulation.

"Why can't you tell me the truth about this baby, Daisy? Why won't you tell me I'm the father?"

Fear. She was so afraid what it would mean to her life if she did. What it would mean to her baby's life. She needed to know how Ryder felt about her, yet she couldn't ask. She wouldn't trap him, and she wouldn't beg for his love. And while last night had been special to her, she could never substitute desire for love, either.

Afraid she'd admit something she shouldn't, afraid Ryder would see the love growing in her heart and feel sorry for her, she turned away from him. "Tell Cade and Leanne I wasn't hungry. I'm going upstairs."

"You're hiding."

Maybe she was, but for now it was the best option.

After Daisy left the kitchen, Ryder slammed his fist down on the counter. "Damn!" Every time he felt he was making headway…

Cade appeared in the doorway. "Sorry if I let the cat out of the bag."

"I'm just sorry Rand noticed no lights up here last night."

"He's keeping an eye on you," Cade responded.

"As a brother should," Ryder said with a sigh.

After a reflective glance at Ryder, Cade went to the cupboard for a glass. "I've been thinking about something this past week. You know, there's still the foundation of a house I was building on Dad's ranch. I have to make up my mind what to do about it."

Last spring Cade had begun the construction of the house as well as negotiations to buy a small plot of land adjacent to their family's spread in Gilas, Texas. He'd been engaged to marry then. But shortly before Garrett called the reunion in Montana, Cade's fiancée had gotten cold feet and called off the wedding. He'd left it all behind to get away from it and to forget when he'd come to Garrett's reunion and then stayed. Since his marriage to Leanne and his decision to take over the horse breeding operation at the Kincaid ranch, his life was here now.

"What are you going to do with it?" Ryder asked.

"I don't know. Maybe *you'd* like to have a place to settle down."

Settle down. The words came more easily to him now. Whenever he thought about Daisy and the baby, he even seemed to like the idea. "She still won't admit I'm the father."

"You two are a lot friendlier than you were a couple of weeks ago."

"I want more than friendly," Ryder muttered.

"Then I guess you'll just have to keep trying to show her that, and hope she comes around."

Cade was right. He'd gotten this far with patience, and patience would take him the rest of the way.

Rays of early sunlight glanced off the snow on Friday morning as Rand guided the draft horses that pulled the hay wagon fixed with snow runners. Ryder rode in the back with Gil Watts. He and Gil hadn't spoken to each other since the night of the fight. With Daisy on Ryder's mind now—she'd kept her distance since Sunday—he could care less what Gil did or said as they cut ropes from the bales and let the hay tumble to the ground. Each bale weighed at least three hundred pounds, and as Ryder's muscles ached from the effort and the cold, he thought about Daisy's hands on his shoulders a few weeks ago. A fantasy took shape and warmed him as the wagon slid through the snow.

Automatically coiling the ropes he'd cut from the hay, Ryder threw them to the rear of the wagon. His fingers were almost frozen but he kept working them to keep the circulation going. As they turned near to at least fifty head of cattle, Gil worked on the other side of the wagon. Eager to get to the feed, the cows came after them.

Gil was standing at the back edge of the wagon, ready to cut the rope and toss the next bale. But somehow—whether he got caught in the rope or simply lost his footing—he went over the back. The bale landed on top of him and the rope caught on the corner of the wagon, dragging both him and the bale.

Ryder shouted, not knowing if Rand would hear him, and jumped off the back with his knife. Adrenaline rushing fast, instincts working overtime, he slashed the rope to keep Gil and the bale from dragging farther, then heaved the bale off of Gil.

Gil was practically buried in the snow and Ryder was worried the cowboy was seriously hurt. Kneeling beside him, he ordered, ''Don't move.''

The horses stopped and Rand came running back as well as he could in the deep snow.

Gil looked dazed, but he pushed himself up to a sitting position, moving first his arms, then his legs. He stared up at Ryder. "I think I'm all right, thanks to you." He looked amazed.

"Thanks to the snow," Ryder responded. "It probably cushioned you enough to keep the full weight of the hay off of you." He remembered Rand always had his cell phone tucked in his pocket to keep in touch with the other men. "We can call for—"

Gil shook his head as Rand trudged to the other side of him. "Let me try to get up."

Rand said, "Gil, I agree, we should get some help."

But Gil shook his head again. "I'm okay. I can tell." Then he pushed himself to his feet before Rand or Ryder could support him.

Facing the man he'd fought a little more than a week ago, Ryder suggested, "You'd better ride up front with Rand. I'll toss the rest of these. When we get back, we'll call the doc to get you checked out just to make sure you're okay."

Gil was still staring at Ryder. "You didn't have to do that. You could have let me drag. You could have let me…suffer."

"That's not my way," Ryder said simply.

As if he couldn't meet Ryder's eyes anymore, Gil looked down at the ground for a few moments, then raised his head and held out his hand. "Thanks."

At that moment Ryder's upbringing as well as his nature took over, and he clasped Gil's hand and shook it.

* * *

When Daisy returned from the reservation on Friday morning, the sun was almost blinding. She wondered where Ryder was. He must have eaten breakfast down at the bunkhouse because he'd been nowhere around when she'd gotten up. She was miserable with the tension between them, but scared of it not being there.

As she hung her coat in the closet, the phone was ringing and no one answered it. Hurrying to the kitchen, she picked it up on the fourth ring. "Kincaid ranch."

"I'd like to speak to Miss Daisy Harding."

"This is she." She thought she recognized the voice...

"Miss Harding, it's Elmer Gladden."

Her principal. Her *former* principal.

He went on, "I know you probably don't want to speak with me, but I have an offer to make you."

"What type of offer?"

"The board met last night and we'd like you to come back and finish out the year with us. The truth is, we can't find someone to replace you. The teachers are complaining that the work you did is being compromised and so, for the good of the children here, we'd like you to reconsider your decision to leave and finish the term."

"I'm still pregnant, still unmarried."

"We've decided your expertise in reading is more important."

"I've found work, Mr. Gladden."

"Oh, I see. A full-time position?"

"No, it's consulting work."

There was a short silence. "Please think about our offer, Miss Harding. We could make the salary worth your while.'' He named a sum that startled her. ''Give it some thought and then let me know. I'll look forward to your call.''

After Daisy hung up, she thought about his offer. The salary he'd offered was too large to not consider. But she was truly enjoying her work on the reservation, and she didn't know if she wanted to give that up. On the other hand, returning to Sedgemore would be the perfect opportunity to put distance between her and Ryder.

Is that what she really wanted?

Later that afternoon, she was still thinking about it—about her session in front of the board before she'd left, the gossip, innuendos and critical looks she was sure she'd suffer if she went back to Sedgemore—when Leanne came in for a few minutes to tell her what had happened between Gil Watts and Ryder. Everyone seemed to be surprised at how Ryder had come to Gil's aid. But Daisy wasn't. That's the kind of man Ryder was.

At supper that night she wanted to bring it up, but she didn't want to make Ryder feel uncomfortable.

When they were almost finished eating, Cade addressed his brother. ''Leanne and I are going down to the barn with the new horses. You still want to go to the Black Boot later with the rest of the men?''

Ryder nodded. ''I'll help Daisy clear up here if you and Leanne want to go down now.''

Cade's brows arched, but he didn't say anything.

After Leanne and Cade had gone, Ryder helped Daisy clear the table and load the dishwasher. He was hanging the towel on the oven handle when she crossed to him.

"I heard what happened today." She couldn't keep the emotion out of her voice.

His gaze passed over her face and rested on her lips. "Just what did you hear?"

"That you saved Gil's life."

Ryder shook his head. "Somebody's exaggerating. I just helped him out of the snow."

This cowboy who could be absolutely exasperating could also be unselfishly humble. "No, you did more than that. You might have made a friend out of an enemy. Is that why you're going out later?"

Ryder's brown eyes darkened. "Watts asked if I wanted to come along with the rest of the men. It seemed like a good idea to say yes."

"I admire you, Ryder," she said softly, meaning it.

Stepping closer to her, he asked, "Do you admire me enough to forgive me for not telling you about the generator on Saturday?" His voice was as serious as it could get.

Maybe some honesty would clear the air between them. "Why did you 'forget' to tell me about the generator? Really."

Taking her hands in his, he held them firmly and smoothed his thumbs over her palms. "I didn't want to spend the evening in separate parts of the house. I wanted to get closer to you and knew if I tried, you might run."

"I'm not running now," she murmured, knowing she loved him more than she could ever have imagined loving a man.

His eyes lit with a blazing fire she wanted to be part of. When he took her into his arms, she knew she wouldn't resist or run this time. Ryder's kiss was so gentle, she almost wanted to cry. He brushed his lips over hers, back and forth a few times, until she moved her lips after his to try to catch him.

Pulling back slightly, he asked, "Are you sure you want this, Daisy? Stopping is so damn hard."

"I don't want you to stop. Not this time. I—"

"Do you know what you're saying?" he asked hoarsely.

She felt her cheeks get hot, and she realized she'd just propositioned him. She was pregnant. He might not even want—

He gripped her shoulders. "Don't you run from me now, Daisy. What are you thinking? That I don't want you? I haven't stopped wanting you since Cade and Leanne's wedding. And if you give me a chance, I'll prove it."

"But I'm pregnant."

"Are you afraid we'll hurt the baby?"

"No, but...I don't look the same."

"The same as what? You're beautiful, Daisy. You were beautiful in September and you're beautiful now."

"Oh, Ryder."

The invitation in her voice must have been his undoing. With a groan, he pulled her to him for a hard, long, intense kiss and before she realized what she intended, he'd scooped her up into his arms.

"What are you doing?" she asked as soon as she could manage it.

"Making sure you won't run away from me." Then he carried her upstairs.

In Ryder's room, he closed the door with his foot and set her down by the bed. "I'd like to undress you," he said in a voice that seduced Daisy as much as the desire in his eyes.

Unable to speak, she just nodded.

Lifting her sweater up and over her head, he tossed it onto the bedside chair. Then he brushed the ends of her hair from her shoulders. "I like your hair like this. I've dreamed of mussing it."

That made her smile. "Like I've dreamed of running my fingers through yours?"

He groaned. "You're not going to make this easy, are you?"

"Do you want it easy?" Heavens, was she flirting with him? Her?

"I want it *good*. For both of us. And it will be, Daisy, I promise you that."

He unclasped her bra, then ran his hands over her breasts, appreciating their fullness. With great reverence, he passed his hand over her stomach, letting it linger there. After he stripped her of the rest of her clothes, he undressed himself and they lay side by side.

She suddenly felt very pregnant, very self-conscious, and avoided his gaze. But he propped himself on one elbow and commanded her, "Look at me, Daisy."

When she turned toward him, he slipped his hand under her hair and brought her to him for a kiss—the kind of kiss she'd never known. It held hunger and longing and maybe even promise.

It was every good thing she'd ever experienced, every wish she'd imagined, every thrill she'd dreamed of. As he ended it, their breathing was ragged and their bodies hot. The small light he'd turned on at the dresser cast a dim glow. "I want to kiss you every-where, Daisy. Everywhere."

Then he started. She trembled, and the room seemed to shake.

When he nibbled on her earlobe, she caught her breath and explored his shoulders. As his lips moved to her neck, she ran her hands up his chest, loving the feel of his hot skin, loving the feel of *him*. She'd never dreamed a man could make her feel this beautiful. She'd never dreamed that Ryder could want her this much. He tasted her collarbone, the valley between her breasts, and then his mouth was on her nipple and she cried out from wanting, from joy, from the sheer pleasure. As he suckled, increasing the amazing sensations in her body, he passed his hands over her skin, drawing moans from her, making her quiver. She couldn't begin to tell him what he was doing to her. She couldn't begin to tell him how much she loved him. But she could show him.

"Give *me* a chance," she said breathlessly.

He pulled away slightly. "A chance for what?"

"A chance to make you feel good."

He laughed. "I'm feeling *very* good."

She could see he was fully aroused, but that wasn't enough. She wanted to be something to him no woman had ever been. "I want to give you pleasure, too."

Stroking through her hair, he murmured, "You can do whatever you want with me, Daisy. Anything."

The thought gave her pause, and she wasn't sure where to begin. But she knew if she watched his expression, and the rise and fall of his breathing, she'd see if she was pleasing him or not. Remembering Saturday night, and his reaction when she'd touched his nipple, she started there.

Slowly she teased her hand up the middle of his chest and when he sucked in a breath, she knew he enjoyed it. With her thumb, she traced around the dark brown nub, then brushed over it. He closed his eyes and his breaths came faster. Bending her head, she touched the nipple with the tip of her tongue. His body tensed.

When she raised her head, he gave her a crooked smile. "If you give me too much pleasure, this is going to be over too soon."

"How much is too much?" she asked innocently.

"We're almost there," he muttered, then kissed her again, sweeping her mouth with his tongue, thrusting in and out, anticipating what was to come next.

His hands were on her again, and they seemed to send pleasure everywhere. She was shaking from the extent of it, yearning for him to join his body to hers.

"Ryder," she said pleadingly.

His voice was hoarse. "I want to make sure you're ready." After he stroked her thighs again, he slid his hand between them and touched her.

She knew she was ready. She wanted him with her heart and her mind and her body and her soul.

Pulling her to him, he nudged her leg up over his hip. "I want to make sure I don't hurt you."

"You won't," she assured him.

When she felt him against her, she arched toward him. He slid into her with excruciating slowness that took her breath away, then began a steady rhythm that had her clutching his shoulders, lacing her hands in his thick hair, giving herself to him completely. The sensations seemed otherworldly, beyond the physical, until she felt as if she'd burst into a million pieces, all of them sparkling and glistening around her, melding her to Ryder in a truly remarkable way she would never forget. She heard him cry her name as he shuddered into her again and again and again. They clasped each other tightly as if neither of them ever wanted to let the other go.

Their breathing had almost returned to normal when a voice called up the stairs, "Ryder, are you up there?"

Ryder swore. "It's Cade. I've got to answer him or he might come up." Kissing Daisy on the forehead, he pulled away from her and went to the door and opened it a crack. "I'm getting dressed. Be down in a few minutes."

Coming back to the bed, he sat beside Daisy. "I'd rather stay here with you."

"I'd rather you stayed here with me, but I know it's important for you to go tonight."

"It is, and it might be pretty late when I get back."

"Tomorrow's another day." She understood that he needed to get a couple of hours' sleep before getting up early in the morning.

"And tomorrow night's another night," he promised her.

She took pleasure in watching him dress, and after he did, he came back to her for a long kiss. When he left the room and closed the door behind him, she thought about making love with him and how wonderful it had been.

What if she told him how she felt? What if she told him she loved him? What if she told him the baby was his?

* * *

When the cowhands from the Kincaid ranch piled into the Black Boot, some went to the booths and some to the tables. A few sat at the stools at the bar. Gil called out that he was buying drinks all around. Gil looked at Ryder kind of funny when he ordered a root beer, but didn't comment.

Ryder had driven a group of them over, and he wasn't about to mix driving with booze and getting up early in the morning. He noticed right away that Jimmy had taken a seat at the bar and seemed to be separated from all the others. The young hand still seemed to blame Ryder for not keeping his secret. Ryder didn't know how the news had gotten out and wished he could bridge the gap between them.

Tonight he just wanted everything to be right with the world. He couldn't believe how he'd felt again with Daisy. When they'd joined, his world had been complete in some way that it hadn't been before. It was an experience he'd never had with a woman— but not one to analyze for too long. He was just looking forward to tomorrow, to seeing her again, and to tomorrow night when maybe she'd come to his room. Surely she'd tell him about the baby then. Surely he could claim his fatherhood.

Her words from earlier in the evening still rang in his head. *I admire you, Ryder.*

It was as if she was saying he could be a good parent, that he *could* be a role model.

As the waitress brought the drinks to the table, Cade tapped Ryder's elbow. "Looks as if someone's staring at you pretty hard."

Glancing at the door, Ryder saw that the woman who'd come in was Marita. Cursing to himself, he realized he never should have flirted with her. He never should have asked her out to the ranch. He never should have acted as if he were free. Because from the moment he'd taken Daisy Harding to bed in September, he hadn't been.

Hanging her jacket on one of the hooks at the front of the honky-tonk, Marita sauntered back to the table where he sat, her skintight red sweater and black jeans made for looking.

A slow song was playing on the jukebox and peering down at Ryder, with a seductive smile, she asked, "How about a dance, cowboy?"

This was the last thing he needed right now. "That's not a good idea tonight, Marita," he said. "But I'm flattered you asked."

"You know what? I think you just need a little convincing," she responded, and she sat on his lap, lacing her arms around his neck. "Maybe this will get you revved up."

Her cloud of perfume assaulted him first as she pressed her lips to his. The idea of kissing any woman other than Daisy absolutely repulsed him, but he didn't want to make a scene, and he didn't want to insult Marita when this was as much his fault as anybody's.

Still, he pulled back quickly and said in a low but firm voice, "There's someone else, Marita. I'm taken."

A short grunt of surprise came from Cade.

Marita stared into his eyes. "*I* don't care, if *you* don't."

He'd always cared about loyalty, and now he realized he cared about fidelity, too. "But I *do* care. That's the point."

After a pout, then a coy smile, she stood. Leaning

down to him, she whispered in his ear, "The lady's lucky. If you ever want my name in your book, just let me know."

At that precise moment, Ryder knew he didn't want any woman's name in his book, except for Daisy's.

Thirteen

Daisy couldn't keep from smiling as she dressed the next morning. Making love with Ryder had been so wonderful. She couldn't wait to see him again. She couldn't wait to tell him about the baby. She was so in love with him, she knew that somehow everything would work out. The way he'd made love to her... He had to care deeply about her, too. It had been obvious in every touch, in every kiss, in every soft whisper.

But she knew she probably wouldn't see him until evening. It seemed like forever to wait. She'd go down to the barn and find Jimmy. They were supposed to have a tutoring session tonight, and she was hoping they could do it right after supper, rather than later, so she could spend the rest of the evening with Ryder.

Maybe tonight she and Ryder could talk about the future. Would Ryder think about settling down? If he didn't, what would she do? If she knew he loved her, it didn't matter where she was. She'd make a home for them—a home he'd want to come back to.

A warning voice in her head told her she was weaving dreams prematurely. She still didn't know where Ryder stood on any of it. But last night had encouraged her to hope in the future again.

The sky was gray, and Daisy had heard the forecast

for more snow. But she and Ryder could be plenty warm... When she thought about tonight, she couldn't wait for it to come.

At the barn, Daisy found Jimmy mucking out stalls. He looked up when he heard her footsteps, and then, without even a greeting, he looked down again at what he was doing.

"Morning, Jimmy. I wanted to set up a time for our session tonight."

"Anytime's okay," he mumbled, still not looking up.

"Is something wrong?" she asked gently.

"No, ma'am."

"Did you go out with the hands last night?" she asked, wondering if they were out late and he was just tired. She hadn't heard Ryder come in.

"Yeah, I did."

"Did you have fun?" It was unusual not to be able to engage Jimmy in conversation.

"No."

"Jimmy, what's wrong? Did something happen?"

He looked up at her then, and she didn't understand the turmoil she saw in his eyes. "Nothing happened. Nothing."

"You seem upset about something."

"I don't know what to do."

"About what?"

"You like Ryder, don't you?"

"Yes, I do. Very much."

Jimmy shook his head. "He was there last night."

"Yes, I know. Nothing happened again between him and Gil, did it?"

"No."

"Apparently *something* happened," she pressed, worried now.

"I don't want to make you upset, but I think you should know…"

"Jimmy, you know you can tell me anything."

He studied her for a few moments. "You've been kind to me, Miss Daisy. You need to know. Ryder was kissing another woman last night."

Daisy's heart skipped a beat, and she stared at Jimmy, stunned.

"It was Marita," he went on in a low voice. "The blonde who was out here."

Daisy could hardly push the question past the lump in her throat. But somehow she managed it. "Where did this happen?"

"At the Black Boot. Everybody saw it."

"Everybody?"

"Yeah. I thought about keeping my mouth shut."

The shock inside of her gave way to a sense of betrayal, disappointment, and then anger. "I'm glad you didn't."

"Are you okay? You look kind of white."

No, she definitely was *not* okay. Everything she'd been thinking this morning proved she was foolish, inexperienced, and terribly naive. A leopard didn't change his spots. How could she have thought for a moment that Ryder would?

She'd given him everything she was last night, but that didn't mean that he was ready to give her anything. She'd compounded her first mistake by making an even bigger one. But now it was time to pull herself together and choose the right road instead of the wrong one. "Jimmy, about our session tonight…I'm not going to be here. I'm going back to Sedgemore as soon as I pack. I know you want to keep up your reading lessons—and you need to—so maybe on the weekends Leanne can drive you to Sedgemore to work with me. Or I can find someone else here who can help you.''

''You're leaving?''

''Yes, I have to. I'll be in touch with you. I promise.''

''Miss Daisy…''

She felt tears starting to burn in her eyes, and she didn't want Jimmy to see her cry. She didn't want him to think this was his fault, because it wasn't. ''I'll see you soon,'' she said, and then turned and almost ran out of the barn.

After tending to the new calves, Ryder decided to make a stop up at the house before he took the colts to the training arena for a workout. He hadn't gotten any sleep last night, thinking about Daisy in the room next door, wanting to go to her, replaying what had happened with Marita. The knowledge that Daisy was the only woman he wanted in his life had been a revelation. But he hadn't gone to her because he needed to tell her about Marita's kiss in the light of day; he needed to tell her that it had meant nothing.

Would she understand that?

The point was, he had to be honest with her.

When he went in the front door, no one else was around. He called Daisy's name, but didn't find her downstairs. As he stood at the foot of the steps, he thought he heard movement in her room. Mounting the stairs quickly, he strode down the hall and found her standing by the bed, packing her suitcase.

''What's going on?'' he asked.

"I'm going back to Sedgemore."

"Now?"

"Yes, now."

"Why?"

She lifted her chin and straightened her shoulders. "Because there's nothing to keep me here."

Nothing to keep her here? "What about last night?"

"Last night?" she asked as if it had meant nothing. "Last night was a lot of fun. But Mr. Gladden called. He wants me to come back. The money's great, so I'm going back, and I'll probably marry the father of my child."

Her words were a blow he couldn't seem to absorb. "Marry the father?"

"Yes, the man who made this baby with me. I'm going to go back to Sedgemore and have a life, Ryder. So I guess this is goodbye."

What the hell had she been doing here? Making up her mind? Comparing him to whoever this other fellow was? Apparently he hadn't measured up. Apparently he wasn't the father of this baby. Apparently he'd been a total fool—once more. "So all these weeks you were making up your mind about what you wanted to do?"

"Yes. That's why I came here. That's what I've done."

Slapping his hat on his head, he decided Daisy Harding would never see that she'd gotten to him. She'd never see that he felt as if the bottom had dropped out of his world. "You have a good life, Daisy. I hope you'll be real happy." Then he headed for the hall and the stairs, knowing he needed to take Lady Luck out for a ride, snow or no snow.

*   *   *

Hardly able to see through her tears, Daisy left a note for Leanne and took her suitcase to her car. No one was around when she left, so she didn't have to make any explanations, and that was just as well. She couldn't explain what an idiot she'd been, how gullible, that she'd fallen in love with a man who didn't know the first meaning of the word.

Snow was falling again as she drove down the access road, then headed for Sedgemore. A fine coating of white settled on layers still not melted by the bright sunshine the day before. A rut jarred the old SUV, and she kept her eyes peeled straight ahead, tears still falling down her cheeks.

She'd reached the outskirts of Whitehorn when she realized she'd have to call Cora Tallbird to tell her she wouldn't be coming back to the school on Laughing Horse. Tears fell even harder as she tried to look ahead rather than back, but she kept remembering Ryder's face as he made love to her, kept remembering the feel of his hands, kept remembering his body joined to hers. Blanking it all out seemed impossible. Pulling a tissue from the box under her radio, she tried to blow her nose with one hand while keeping the vehicle steady. The road stretched ahead of her like the rest of her life, and she couldn't believe her sense of desolation, the terrible cloud of loneliness, the awful sense of betrayal.

She was staring straight ahead, trying to blink her tears away when, out of nowhere, a deer pranced onto the road. She couldn't hit it, she couldn't. Reacting instinctively, she swerved. Her vehicle slid and skidded into the snow mounds on the side of the road.

The last thing she heard was the scrunch of metal into ice-slick snow as her head hit the steering wheel.

Riding Lady over the packed roads that had been plowed to get feed to the cattle, Ryder tried to breathe through the piercing ache in his chest. He'd tried to shut off his mind as he'd ridden into the cold and the snow. Lost in soul-deep devastation, his thoughts had gotten buried under the god-awful ache of losing something he'd wanted badly. Wanted. It wasn't simply a matter of want. It was a matter of need. It was a matter of...

Love.

The thought, let alone the word, shocked him, but he realized with all-too-certain clarity he loved Daisy Harding, but she obviously didn't love him.

She'd never said he was the father. She'd never said she hadn't slept with another man. She'd never said anything about how she felt. But last night...

Last night. She'd been all soft and glowing and tender and radiant. What had happened?

As snow fell harder, he realized *something* had. Some women's moods might change like quicksilver, but Daisy's didn't. She was usually calm and quiet unless something specific got her dander up, unless something specific upset her. What had made her decide to pack and leave today? A call from the principal where she'd taught?

He supposed it was possible. But that idea didn't feel right. It didn't feel right at all. Somebody had to know what was going on. Somebody had to know why she'd suddenly decided to leave.

If she hadn't left yet, he'd kiss the reasons out of

her and he'd tell her how he felt. And if there was another man…?

Whatever was going on, Ryder would deal with it. If Daisy loved him, they could solve anything.

When Ryder got back, he took care of Lady, and then went to check the garage. Daisy's car was gone. He swore viciously, and then headed for the training arena where Leanne was working. Maybe she'd know something. On the way there, he spotted Jimmy leading one of the colts to the arena.

"Did you talk to Daisy before she left?" Ryder asked him.

The young hand looked startled. "Did she really leave?"

"Her car is gone. I'm trying to find out why she decided to go back to Sedgemore so quickly."

Jimmy avoided Ryder's eyes for a moment, then said, "I know why."

"Why?"

"I told her something."

Ryder waited.

"She's been good to me, Ryder. I didn't want to see you do her dirty. Not like you did me. I told her you kissed Marita last night."

No curse seemed adequate enough. "Why would you do such a thing?" he exploded. "Why would you interfere? I didn't do *anything* to you, Jimmy. I don't know who found out about your reading problem, but I didn't say a word. And for you to upset Daisy like this—"

A yell came from the barn, and Cade came out of the door at a dead run toward Ryder. "It's Daisy. She was in an accident. The hospital in Whitehorn called. She wants Leanne—"

"No." Ryder cut him off. "*I'm* going. How serious is it?"

"They didn't give me any details."

Ryder swore again.

"It's my fault," Jimmy said, sounding near tears.

But Ryder shook his head and capped the young man's shoulder. "It's *not* your fault. If this is anybody's fault, it's mine." Then he ran to his truck, knowing he had to get to her, hoping he could put everything right, praying it wasn't too late.

The ride to Whitehorn Memorial Hospital was the longest of Ryder's life. After he parked, he rushed into the emergency room, figuring that's where she'd be, all the while praying, Please, God, let her be all right. Please, God, let the baby be okay.

When he asked for Daisy at the desk, the nurse looked him up and down. "Are you related?"

"I'm going to marry her," he said.

At that, she lead him back to a cubicle, where he saw Daisy lying on a gurney, looking pale. Rushing over to her, he asked, "Are you all right? Is the baby all right?"

She seemed surprised to see him, and a guarded look came into her eyes as she sat up. "I'm fine. The baby's fine." Her hand went to the gauze patch on her forehead. "I had a few stitches."

He was still trying to sort everything out in his head, trying to find all the words he needed to use. To stall for a little more time, he asked, "What happened?"

"It was a deer. He ran out in front of me and I swerved to miss him. I bumped my head on the steering wheel. I guess I blacked out for a few minutes, and they wanted to make sure I didn't have a concussion. But the doctor says everything looks okay.''

"Thank God,'' Ryder breathed, then took her hand in his and sat by her hip. "Daisy, look. I'm not sure how to say this. There are so many things I want to say. But I love you. And it's not because of the baby.''

The disbelief in her eyes hurt him.

"I *do* love you. Jimmy told me what he said to you. I was going to tell you about last night.''

Her eyes glistened, and she shook her head as if she didn't want to hear any of it.

But he kept hold of her hand. "Jimmy was sitting at the bar, and he couldn't hear what went on at our table. But Cade did. Marita asked me if I wanted to dance. I told her no. But then she sat on my lap and laid a kiss on me before I could stop her. After she did, I told her there was someone else. I told her I was taken. You can ask Cade if you won't believe me.''

Daisy's gaze locked to his, and it was as if she was trying to read every thought in his mind, every feeling in his heart, every corner of his soul.

"I love you, Daisy,'' he said again, determined to convince her. "I know I'm only a cowboy. I know I'm not educated like you are. But I can't imagine a life without you, and I promise I'll spend every day proving how much you mean to me. Is there really another man you want to marry?'' He couldn't bear the thought, but he had to face reality so he could deal with it.

Tears rolled down her cheeks, and she shook her head. "There's no other man. There's only you. And, Ryder, I *love* you being a cowboy. That's who you are. You're wise in so many ways that don't have anything to do with going to school. I love you so much…'' Her voice caught, and she took a breath. "I think I've loved you since…since September. And this baby is yours."

He'd longed to hear those words for so many weeks that he could hardly believe they were true. But the glowing joy in Daisy's eyes told him they were. Any insecurity he'd had fled when he saw the respect, admiration and love so alive in her eyes. Gathering her into his arms, he held her for a time, then finally sealed his lips to hers. The kiss went on and on and on. Neither of them could get enough, neither of them wanted to end it, neither of them ever wanted to be separated again.

"It's about time," Leanne said from the doorway.

"When's the wedding?" asked Cade.

Ryder tried to slow the beat of his heart, but it seemed hopeless as he lifted his head, placed a kiss on Daisy's forehead and turned to his brother and sister-in-law. "Do you think you could give us a few minutes so I could propose like I should?"

Cade grinned at his brother, wrapped his arm around his wife, and led her away from the door.

Then Ryder took Daisy's hand in his again and looked deep into her eyes. "I'm going to quit the rodeo circuit, and I'd like to settle in Texas in the house Cade started to build. I'm going to take it over from him. Will you marry me and share a life with me there?"

Daisy entwined her fingers with his, then reached up and stroked his jaw. "I'll marry you and make a life with you wherever you want to be."

Taking her into his arms, Ryder kissed her again,

knowing he'd found the perfect woman for him, knowing he'd found the love of his life, knowing their future would be happier than anything he'd experienced in his past. Daisy Harding was the woman he'd been looking for all his life, and he was never going to let her go.

Epilogue

Purple, pink, blue and gold streaks of color painted the evening sky as Ryder and Daisy walked around the foundation of a ranch house. Ryder made sure Daisy's arm was carefully tucked into his. The turned-up earth was uneven, and he didn't want her to stumble. She was getting rounder by the day. He remembered how she'd looked on their wedding day only a month ago and thought she looked even prettier now. But then he guessed he was a bit biased.

His wife turned toward him, her eyes shining with love. "When Leanne called this morning, she said Jimmy read her a story he'd written. Lynn Garrison's been spending Saturday afternoons tutoring him, and he's making great progress. Even the hands respect his ability to stick to it. Gil offered to take him for his driver's test when he's ready."

Daisy had found a tutor for Jimmy before they'd left Montana. "You miss all of them, don't you?" Ryder asked.

"Yes, but I love being here, too, getting to know your parents, making new friends."

"We'll go up and visit after the baby's born."

"You might be too busy," she warned.

Ryder had decided he liked spending time with kids almost as much as with horses. He and Daisy had spent long hours into the night, making love but talk-

ing about the future, too. And in the week before
they'd come to Texas for the wedding, he'd decided
he wanted to open a training camp on the land he'd
purchased. He'd train horses, but he'd also teach kids
how to ride and how to handle their animal. It was
fulfilling work that he knew would go well with having a family, with setting a course for the future. "I
won't be too busy to show off my son or daughter."

Daisy laughed. "I think you're going to have to
fight with your mom and dad to get the chance to do
it."

Ryder's parents had been overjoyed at the news he
was settling down, and they already loved Daisy and
Leanne, claiming they were daughters now, not
daughters-in-law. Finding love had made everything
in Ryder's life fall into place. He slid his arm around
his wife. "This will be a fine house." He could already imagine the walls and windows and roof.

"It'll be a home."

Ryder brought her into the circle of his arms.
"We'll make it a home filled with love—beginning
with ours. Do you know how much I love you?"

Her sweet smile thrilled him and aroused him and
urged him to give thanks again for her. "I think I'm
beginning to," she murmured. "Do you know how
much I love *you?*"

Everyday she showed him in so many ways. "I'm
beginning to," he responded with a smile of his own.

They'd spent many nights, before their wedding
and after, talking into the morning hours. He'd told
her about Sandra, how he couldn't seriously commit
to any woman before because he wasn't sure of his
own worth. It had been hard to admit. But Daisy had
understood. Once she'd confided in him about her

parents' marriage, he'd understood her fears about loving and believed with her secret, she was truly giving him her trust.

Daisy tightened her arms around his neck. "I think we should renew our wedding vows at least once a year."

Resting his forehead against hers, he decided, "I think we should do it every day."

"Are you turning into a romantic?"

"Uh-uh. Just a man in love."

"Oh, Ryder…"

When she said his name like that, he had to kiss her. And with the kiss, he promised all over again to honor, love and cherish her for the rest of their lives.

MONTANA BRIDES
continues next month with

THE BIRTH MOTHER
by Pamela Toth

and
RICH, RUGGED...RUTHLESS
by Jennifer Mikels.

Turn the page for an exciting preview
of THE BIRTH MOTHER...

The Birth Mother

by

Pamela Toth

As Emma Stover locked the front door of the Hip Hop Café and turned to the sidewalk, the figure of a man appeared suddenly, blocking her path. The streetlight was behind him, shadowing his face as he confronted her.

Frightened, Emma clutched the keys like a weapon and opened her mouth to scream.

"I've been waiting for you," the man said, turning slightly so the light caught the side of his face.

"Brandon!" she yelped in relief, her knees nearly buckling as she clapped her free hand over her thundering heart. "You scared the heck out of me!"

Brandon Harper caught her arms as she swayed. "Damn, I'm sorry. I only meant to surprise you. Are you okay?"

"Yes, of course." Embarrassed, Emma managed a weak laugh as he let her go. Her glasses had slid down her nose, so she pushed them back up as she stared.

Even in the poor light, black-haired Brandon's angular face was devilishly attractive. He towered over Emma, making her feel ridiculously petite instead of just boringly average in height. The other waitresses teased her when he came in to eat, insisting he sat at her station deliberately, but she hadn't seen him in weeks. For some reason he'd been on her mind today as she pictured the quiet intensity of his gaze and the sensual curve of his mouth. She'd wondered whether she would ever see him again and now here he was as though she'd conjured him up herself.

She was so relieved that she wanted to touch him to make sure he was real. "I'm sorry," she said instead, tucking the keys into the pocket of her uniform shorts. "I don't usually close up by myself, so I guess I was a little nervous. I didn't mean to overreact."

"Don't apologize," Brandon replied, his deep voice as smooth as the surface of a lake on a still evening. "I was the one who should have had more sense than to jump out at you the way I did."

"Why are you here?" Emma blurted.

His teeth flashed white in the gloom. "To see you, of course."

For a moment she felt like Red Riding Hood in the presence of the wolf. The last time he'd come into the café he asked her to join him on her break. She'd enjoyed talking to him, but she'd also understood that he was only passing the time with her. Men like Brandon didn't fall for plain-Jane waitresses.

"Would you like to go somewhere for a drink?" he asked, shocking her.

Was it possible he'd been serious about coming to see her? For a moment, Emma was almost unbearably tempted to accept his offer. Then reality hit like a dash of cold water. He was just being polite.

"I'd better not. The café was busy tonight and I'm pretty tired. I wouldn't be very good company."

"Sure, I understand." He raised his head and looked around. "Where did you park? The least I can do is escort you to your car."

Emma noticed his sleek dark sedan sitting alone in

the customer lot like a panther waiting to spring. "I'm parked around back." Instead of pining like a teen with an unrequited crush, she should be grateful he was considerate enough to walk her down the deserted alley.

In silence Emma led the way around the building to where her old green Chevy waited in the shadows. He walked alongside her, grasping her elbow briefly when she stumbled on the loose gravel. His fingers were warm against her bare skin, but he let her go almost immediately after she mumbled her thanks.

He waited patiently while she unlocked her door and then he held it open for her as she climbed behind the wheel. Flustered by his gallant gesture, she rolled down her window to thank him.

"No problem," he replied, peering at her in the gloom. "Have a good night." He stepped back expectantly.

Her hands were shaking, so it took two tries to find the ignition with her key. When she turned it, nothing happened. Frowning, she jiggled the gearshift lever and tried again.

"Trouble?" Brandon asked.

"It won't start," Emma admitted, fighting sudden tears.

"Let me try." He opened her door. "Slide over."

Quickly she moved over so he could get in beside her. He seemed to fill the interior of the car with his presence, so Emma pressed closer to the passenger door.

The engine was no more responsive to Brandon's touch than it had been to hers. "Maybe it's the battery," he suggested.

"No, it can't be. I just bought a new one."

"I suppose even new batteries can go bad. I'm no mechanic, but I guess I can take a look. Do you have a flashlight?"

When she found one in the glove box, he got out, raised the hood and shone the light over the engine.

"Find anything?" she called through the open window.

"You say you just bought a new battery?" he asked, an odd note in his voice.

"That's right."

"It's not here."

"What?" Emma frowned as his words sank in, and then she scooted out of the car to peer under the hood herself. There was an empty space next to the engine. "It's gone," she said foolishly.

"At least we know why the car wouldn't start." As she stood back, he shut the hood, gave it an experimental tug and switched off the flashlight. "Get your purse and lock the doors. I'll take you home."

"Oh, no, that's not necessary," she babbled. "I can call someone else. I don't want to take you out of your way."

"Don't be silly. I'm not going to leave you here." Brandon sounded impatient, making her feel even worse. "Where do you live?"

It would probably be quicker to agree than to continue arguing. "My apartment's a ten-minute drive."

Except for brief directions, Emma couldn't think of anything to say on the way and Brandon barely spoke. As she sank into the luxurious leather of his Lexus and listened to something low, slow and seductive ooze from his stereo, she wished the short trip would never end.

Too soon he turned onto her street. "It's the next

driveway,'' she said. ''My apartment is over the garage behind the house.'' The street was empty, the neighborhood quiet except for the distant growl of a motorcycle.

Brandon parked on the other side of the garage, away from the house. She'd expected him to wait with the engine running while she went up the stairs to her door. Instead he shut it off and got out of the car.

''Would you like to come in?'' she asked after he had circled the car to let her out. ''The least I can do is to give you a cup of coffee or a glass of iced tea for all your trouble.''

''It was no trouble,'' he replied, ''but something cold to drink does sound good.''

Before Emma knew how it happened, they were seated on the Hide-A-Bed sofa in her tiny apartment and she was explaining why she'd come to Whitehorn. Once she relaxed, talking to Brandon was easy. Perhaps it was because he was such a good listener, his gaze steady on her face as though he found her fascinating.

She didn't usually tell people the truth about herself—that she'd been raised in foster homes—but he wormed it out of her with his questions. Then he dumbfounded her by admitting that he, too, had grown up as a ward of the court. He didn't elaborate, but Emma figured he'd understand her real reason for coming to Whitehorn.

''Three months ago I came here to find my birth mother,'' she blurted. Belatedly she realized she'd been talking his ear off while his glass sat empty. Her cheeks flamed with embarrassment as she leaped to her feet. "I didn't mean to go on like that. Let me refill this."

Before she could escape into her minuscule kitchen with his glass, Brandon stood and blocked her way. "You didn't tell me whether you found her," he said softly, resting his hands on Emma's shoulders to stop her flight.

She stared at the solid wall of his chest and breathed in his scent. "Who?" she asked blankly.

He chuckled. "Your birth mother."

Lifting her gaze to his face, Emma considered what she'd so recently learned about the woman who'd given her life. But just because Emma and Brandon shared a history didn't mean she was prepared to tell him about Lexine Baxter. "I'm getting closer," she hedged.

His grin widened and he squeezed her shoulders. "Good girl. That must make you happy."

She couldn't admit to her mixed emotions without explaining the situation. "It's hard to believe you were a foster child," she said, desperate to change the subject.

He cocked his head. "Why is that?"

His question surprised her. The answer seemed so obvious. "Because you're so—" Flustered, she tried again. "You don't seem—" Why hadn't she kept her mouth shut?

"Yes?"

Emma wriggled from his grasp and ducked around him. "I'll get that iced tea."

Brandon caught up with her in the kitchen before she could open the door of the old-fashioned refrigerator. The room was barely big enough for the two of them. He took the empty glass from her hand and set it down. Stepping back, Emma bumped the counter behind her.

Brandon was watching her with a quizzical smile. "I'm still waiting."

She stared up at him. His haircut alone probably cost more than she cleared in tips in a week. "I can't explain."

He looked disappointed. "I'm just a man, Emma. I laugh, I hurt. I get lonely like everyone else."

She couldn't imagine someone like Brandon Harper being alone unless he wanted it that way. He'd mentioned his family. From what she'd heard about his grandfather Garrett Kincaid, he was a welcoming sort. Was it possible Brandon struggled with the same doubts and insecurities as she did? Not very likely. Before she could think of a way to ask, he leaned closer and his gaze drifted to her mouth.

The air in the kitchen crackled with sudden tension. Emma's eyes widened at the intent in his. "Are you going to kiss me?" she blurted.

"If it's all right with you," he responded gravely.

She swallowed as he cupped her chin with his fingers. Her pulse fluttered erratically. She must have fallen asleep in her car and now she was dreaming.

"Emma? May I?"

"Yes, please," she whispered, realizing that, asleep or awake, she craved Brandon Harper's kiss as much as just about anything else she had ever wanted in her life....

* * * *

Don't forget
THE BIRTH MOTHER *and*
RICH, RUGGED...RUTHLESS
are on the shelves next month.

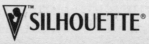

Danger, deception and desire

SILHOUETTE

INTRIGUE™

Enjoy these dynamic mysteries with a
thrilling combination of breathtaking
romance and heart-stopping suspense.
Unexpected plot twists and
page-turning writing will keep you
on the edge of your seat.

Four new titles every month
available from the
READER SERVICE™
on subscription